ETHICS AND SOCIETY

RICHARD T. DE GEORGE is Professor of Philosophy at the University of Kansas. This past year he was Senior Research Fellow and Lecturer at Columbia University and has been a recipient of Fulbright and Ford Foundation fellowships. Professor De George is the editor of *Classical and Contemporary Metaphysics;* he has written a number of articles on Soviet ethics and is the author of *Patterns of Soviet Thought* (1966).

ETHICS AND SOCIETY

*Original Essays on
Contemporary Moral Problems*

BY

HENRY DAVID AIKEN

KURT BAIER

BRAND BLANSHARD

ERROL E. HARRIS

ROBERT O. JOHANN

HERBERT MARCUSE

A. I. MELDEN

CHARLES L. STEVENSON

THOMAS S. SZASZ

EDITED BY RICHARD T. DE GEORGE

Anchor Books
Doubleday & Company, Inc.
Garden City, New York
1966

The Anchor Books edition is the first publication of
*Ethics and Society: Original Essays on
Contemporary Moral Problems*

Anchor Books edition: 1966

PREFACE

Contemporary philosophy seems to many to have become a technical discipline divorced from the problems of society. But the need for the clarity which philosophy can bring to social problems is as great as ever. Questions of civil rights, of international policy, of criminal responsibility are moral as well as social in nature. The present essays constitute an attempt to clarify some basic problems of ethics as well as to bring to bear the moral insights of some noted thinkers on contemporary issues. Together they help us advance one step further along the road society must travel to find solutions to its many problems.

The essays which make up this volume were originally given as lectures in a series sponsored by the Department of Philosophy at the University of Kansas and were made possible by funds from a Ford Foundation grant to the University in support of international studies. The contributors represent some of the different views present in our pluralistic society. Most are professors of philosophy; one is also a Jesuit priest, another a professor of psychiatry. Characteristically no two of them agree fully on the strictly theoretical level. Yet a remarkable unity emerges with respect to specific moral judgments about what is right.

Some of the papers are concerned primarily with conceptual analysis in an attempt to make clear the meanings of basic terms. Others merely sketch ethical positions and attempt to show the relevance of these positions to contemporary problems. Still others grapple directly with a particular moral issue and suggest practical solutions. All three types of endeavor are necessary at every stage of mankind's development, and the three are all interrelated. Practical problems demand solutions; but they are best solved with the aid of clear, viable, consistent theories. Each society and each age must decide for itself what it considers right and good. But the clearer it is about the meaning of these terms and the nature of and basis for its moral judgments, the more intelligently it can proceed.

This volume, then, is premised upon the dual belief that there is a need for philosophical clarity and analysis and that philosophy can be relevant to the practical issues facing contemporary society.

Richard T. De George

CONTENTS

ETHICS AND SOCIETY

MORALITY AND POLITICS

Brand Blanshard

BRAND BLANSHARD is Emeritus Professor of Philosophy at Yale University. He was a Rhodes Scholar (1913–15, 1919–20), a Guggenheim Fellow (1929–30), and President of the Eastern Division of the American Philosophical Association (1942–44). He has delivered the Gifford Lectures at St. Andrews, the Carus Lectures, the Noble and Whitehead Lectures at Harvard, and the Hertz Lecture at the British Academy. He is the author of *The Nature of Thought* (1939), *Reason and Goodness* (1961), and *Reason and Analysis* (1962).

I should like to advance three theses: first, that political thought depends on ethics; second, that the kind of ethics that provides its firmest basis is an ethics of consequences; and third, that conformity to this ethics would make a large difference in our political theory and practice.

First, then, does politics depend on ethics? I think it does. Indeed I submit that all political problems are in the end ethical problems. And by political problems I mean here both the day to day problems faced by the legislator, and the problems of political theory, of how government itself is to be organized or justified. Politics in both these senses depends, I suggest, on ethics.

Take politics in the first and very wide sense, in which any question about what a government should do is a political question. All such questions, or nearly all, are ethical. Any selection from the program of the present Congress, picked out at random, would serve to show this. Shall black men have the same civil rights as white men? That is so

clearly a moral question that the churches, normally re-
luctant to involve themselves in "politics," feel that they cannot afford to do otherwise. What of Medicare? Should old
people who, through improvidence or ill fortune, lack the
means to take care of their health, be supplied with these
means by society? Surely, again a moral question. What of
the war in Viet Nam? That may not look like a moral question at the first glance, but it quickly becomes one if we
think. Suppose we withdraw from that country on condition
that it be neutralized; what would that lead to? Many believe that it would lead to the communization, under Chinese auspices, of all southeast Asia and that this in turn
would threaten the present order in Malaysia and the Philip-
pines, perhaps in the end Australia and the rest of the world.
Suppose these consequences *are* involved; then the problem
whether their net good is to be preferred to the net good of
our staying on is a moral problem of the highest moment.

You may ask, "What makes a problem moral rather
than merely technical or intellectual?" The question is an
interesting one. The words "moral" and "morals" are used
today in many ways. When the morals of Hollywood are discussed, what is commonly meant is sex morals; when the
moral law is discussed, many mean by it the law sanctioned
by their religion. These senses are far too narrow. I should
suggest that any question is a moral question whose decision
depends on a choice between values. A non-moral question
becomes moral the instant values are introduced. Take a simple case. You go to a bank with a ten-dollar check; the teller
asks how will you have it—in a ten-dollar bill, two fives, a five
and five ones, or what? Is this a moral question? No; the
amount will be the same, whatever the combinations are;
what difference does it make which one is chosen? If it really
does make none, then there is nothing moral about the
choice. But suppose it does make some; suppose you reflect
that five minutes later you will be taking a bus to the station,
and that to present a ten-dollar bill to a harried bus driver is
to make oneself a nuisance. Is the choice still a non-moral

one? I think not. To make oneself a nuisance is to choose the lower of two values, and that is always wrong; indeed I am going to argue that this is what "wrong" means. Whether you agree about that or not, I hope you will agree that what makes a choice a moral choice, as opposed to its being outside the sphere of morality, is that it involves increasing or decreasing the values in the world. If you do agree, all values become at least potentially moral. From one point of view, the difference between a box of chocolates and a box of candied orange peel is not moral but gustatory; but if you are meditating on which to give your grandmother on her birthday, and you remember that she abhors chocolates and loves orange peel, that little gustatory difference provides the difference between right and wrong; one cannot decently disregard it.

It is not only the questions of practical politics that are in this sense moral; it is also the great questions of political theory. I am not speaking here of political science, which is a factual study—a study of how governments are in fact constructed and run; I am speaking of political theory, which is the study of how they ought to be constructed and run. It is plain from that word "ought" that political theory is applied ethics. Ought there to be governments at all? Bakunin and Kropotkin, and—under certain conditions—Marx and Tolstoi, thought not. How are you to argue with these anarchists? Surely by trying to show that government is a necessary means to certain great goods, which they want as much as the rest of us. Does a government have a right to limit freedom of speech (as Justice Black denies), to reach into our pockets and take a large part of our income (as Edmund Wilson denies), to make murderers pay with their lives (as Clarence Darrow denied), to limit population in peace by contraception or in war by atomic bombs (as the Catholic Church denies)? There is no convincing way of arguing these issues except by making them questions of comparative value, that is ethical questions. Political theory as well as political practice ends in ethics. "The principles of true poli-

3

tics," said Edmund Burke, "are those of morality enlarged; and I neither now do, nor will ever admit of any other." Lord Acton quoted that passage in his inaugural address at Cambridge, and it will serve as my text.

If what Burke says is true, it is important to the person working in politics that his ethics should be sound. What sort of ethical basis should he stand on? That is the second question I want to raise, and it is of course a vast one. It cannot be answered adequately short of an entire ethical theory, defended against alternative theories. I cannot attempt to produce that, though I am going to venture a sketch of the only ethical theory I think will serve in politics or elsewhere.

But first a warning about two ethical views that are popular today, though I think mistaken and dangerous. One comes from the anthropologists, the other from the positivists. Either one of them would make a political philosophy all but impossible.

The first is a theory that has been imported into our anthropology departments in the knapsacks of their returning field workers. If you have missed your junior year in Paris these days, you can make up for it in some measure by a graduate year or two in Borneo or Papua, where if you interview head-hunters faithfully in their own happy hunting-grounds, you will find them expressing views about marriage, religion, and the other proprieties, which are not those prevailing in the select circles of Lawrence, Kansas. Indeed if you compare notes with a wide enough variety of field workers, you may find that apart from certain leanings toward animism and a disapproval of incest, there is hardly a custom adopted anywhere that is not viewed with repugnance somewhere else. Parents who in China would be treated with reverence are, or recently were, put to death by their children in Fiji; in some parts of Asia unwanted children are quietly disposed of, while in America even abortion is a crime; some communities are ruled by patriarchs and some by matriarchs; marriage varies from the civilized monogamy of the Veddas of Ceylon to the primitivism of Hollywood. What is the lesson of such facts? Our Yale anthropologist Sumner suggested a conclusion that has come in many quarters to seem a truism: "The mores can make anything right"—and he meant not *seem* right but *really* right. If a practice has the approval of a society or culture, then for that society it *is* right; that is all that "right" can legitimately mean. Some group beyond the sea may disapprove it, and for that group it is wrong. But for either of them to dictate to the other is presumption, and to look for some absolute good or right, authoritative for both, is futile. Moral standards are relative, not absolute or universal; this is the voice of humanity, modesty, charity, democracy, sophistication. The ethics of the new age is cultural relativism.

Though this theory was made plausible by anthropologists, it was not invented by them. If one strips it of the vast mass of anthropological facts that now cluster around it, it turns out to be fairly close to the well-known theory of Hume. Hume held that to approve of conduct is to have a certain feeling about it, a feeling caused by its perceived tendency to increase the happiness of people with whom we can sympathize; and to pronounce it right is to say that in our society people generally feel that way about it. Now if approval is favoring or liking, you cannot argue either for or against it; to try to prove or disprove a feeling would be absurd. Morals, therefore, are not a rational affair; if by flicking a finger we could destroy or save the whole of mankind, neither choice, said Hume, would be more rational or irrational than the other. *De gustibus non disputandum;* there is no disputing or refuting a man's taste. The best you can do is to show that his taste is out of line with that of his fellows. This is essentially cultural relativism, the view so persuasively illustrated in Ruth Benedict's *Patterns of Culture.* Miss Benedict, if we can tolerate the image, is David Hume in petticoats.

I have suggested that if you adopt this theory in ethics, you may as well give up in political theory. Why? Because the major fact in the modern world is that cultures are in conflict, with enormous powers of destruction on each side, and this theory affords no rational way of dealing with that conflict. It is idle to say that if the Russians generally think they have no obligation to pay for the enforcement of peace, and Americans think they have, they are both right. That, in practice, means anarchy.

In 1931 the Japanese chose to expand into Manchuria; in 1935 the Italians chose to expand into Ethiopia; in 1939 the Germans swallowed half of Poland. Apparently the people in each case were behind their government, and it follows on the theory before us that the action of the government was right. In each case it was denied that there was any court of higher appeal, legal or moral, that could overrule this verdict. Cultural relativism would leave us no principles by which the issue could be argued or arbitrated, since these would be supracultural principles, not relative to any culture, and we are told there are no such principles. How, then, are these differences to be settled? We know how they have in fact been settled. When a schoolboy was asked what would happen if an irresistible force met an immovable obstacle, he answered, "an inconceivable smash." That is the answer often supplied by history; has cultural relativism anything better to offer? Apparently not. It can of course encourage us all to like each other, to like the same things, and otherwise to reach for the moon. But if there are no supracultural principles by which, even in theory, we can adjudicate our differences, the way is left open for force. This, being approved on both sides, will also be right for both until one destroys the other and renders it morally negligible. That may settle the issue, but it does not solve it; it is mere theoretical bankruptcy.

The other current theory that seems to me a danger is emotivism, which has commended itself to some philosophers as the result of a new test of meaning proposed by the positivists. They say that to find precisely what a statement means, you should ask how you would verify it, and the mode of verification will give you the meaning. Suppose you say that John is blasphemous; how would you test that? By observing whether John repeatedly uses certain words; hence the use of such words is what you mean by his being blasphemous. Suppose now you say that John is a good man, and you try to fix the meaning of good in the same way. You look at his conduct and ask whether he habitually does, or tries to do, right. Excellent; but what do you mean by right acts? The test, you may say, is good consequences, but what do you mean by that? Well, you know that association with John has made you both wiser and happier, and you point to these as the sort of consequences you have in mind. But suppose someone challenges you as to why you call wisdom and happiness good. What exactly do you mean by "good"? Is the goodness of these things some special quality that they have, something that you can observe, as you can roundness or redness? No, apparently not. Their goodness, whatever that is, is something that has never been seen, heard, touched, or otherwise sensed or perceived. But what is unobservable is unverifiable; and if it is unverifiable, the horrid suspicion arises that there is no meaning there to verify. To be sure, when you call something good, you are not just making a noise; you are expressing something; but what you are expressing is feeling or emotive meaning, of the kind expressed by "Cheers!" or "Wow!", or perhaps supplicatory meaning like "Won't you please join in giving a cheer for John?" For positivists and most other analytic thinkers, moral judgments have ceased to be judgments at all; they do not express knowledge of any kind; they are neither true nor false; they are exclamations, commands, or entreaties.

No wonder people speak of a revolution in ethics. If this account is correct, it is more than a revolution, it is an annihilation of traditional ethics. The main interest of ethics has been to find out by thinking what is good, or what is right, or what one ought to do. We are now told that this attempt has been misguided from the beginning. To be sure, we can still inquire how people use ethical words, but that is semantics; we can still dissect the various attitudes of favoring and disfavoring, but that is psychology; we can still study how cultures vary in their feeling about types of behavior, but that is sociology. Ethics as a science has vanished.

If our sole concern here were ethical, I should have much to say on this astonishing view. But I must limit myself to what it implies for political theory. What does it imply? This, I am afraid: that political theory has joined ethics in a suicide pact. For what is political theory? It is a reasoned account of the extent and ground of our political rights and duties. And no such account is now possible. Suppose you take any political right or duty at random and deal with it in the manner of Professor A. J. Ayer in *Language, Truth and Logic*. Mr. Ayer says that the statement "stealing is wrong" is equivalent to "stealing!", where the exclamation point says nothing about the act but only expresses something in the judge, namely a feeling of aversion. Suppose you say, in the same way, "John ought not to have dodged his income tax." To the political thinker the question of interest lies in how you would justify that statement. You are told by the emotivist that you have not said anything true or false, so the request to justify it, if that means showing it to be true, is pointless. Can you offer evidence for it? You can show that most people dislike it, but that too is irrelevant, for the question is whether their dislike is justified. You can show that such conduct naturally leads on to other forms of lawlessness, which you or most people dislike, but then *this* dislike must be justified. Sooner or later you come face to face with a dilemma: if your statement is just an explosion of feeling, you can no more justify it logically than you can prove a headache; on the other hand, if you *can* justify it by argument or evidence, then it is more than a feeling; it is a judgment, a statement that is true or false. Genuine political theory becomes possible only when emotivism has been left behind.

Emotivism was offered to the world before its implications were worked out. When they are worked out, they prove fatal for traditional political theory, but they go even further. Everyone knows that political questions are favorite topics for debate. We are now told that so far as these questions are ethical, they cannot even be debated. Professor Stevenson, whose view is essentially emotivist, holds that when you differ with someone else on a moral issue, your argument must take the form, not of trying to refute him, but of bringing causal influences to bear upon him to change his feeling about the matter. And not only is it impossible to debate the issue; it is impossible even to differ in opinion on it. If you say that John was wrong in evading his tax, and I deny this, neither of us is voicing an opinion at all; we differ only in attitude. It is likewise impossible to *agree* in opinion about it, for we cannot agree in having what neither of us has. Once more, a rational defense of the existence of the state is impossible. The British philosopher R. M. Hare, who thinks that moral judgments are really commands, thinks that you can defend a particular law or custom by showing that it is bound up with a way of life as a whole; that you can argue for granting a high degree of freedom by showing that it is necessary to an individualist order; and that, on the other hand, you can argue that much restriction of freedom is necessary if your ideal order is socialist. The ultimate issue in such an argument, then, is whether one order or way of life as a whole is preferable to another. And that question, Mr. Hare maintains, is incapable of rational settlement; it can be settled only by a commitment of the will. This seems to me very significant. It shows that if you follow to the end the positivists' way of thinking on ethics and politics, or that of their successors, the linguistic analysts, you find them settling the ultimate questions in the manner of their enemies, Kierkegaard and the existentialists, by falling back on a nonrational act of will.

We have so far been concerned with some current ethical views that seem to impose a veto on political philosophy. It is time I showed my own hand. I do hold a position in ethics that seems to me, perhaps through vanity, to have been arrived at by a process of thought, not by an act of faith or will;

and I can plead at least this much for it, that there is very little in it that originated with me. I will put it before you in the briefest and baldest terms, and then try to show its political importance.

Sir David Ross has accustomed us to thinking that the great questions of ethics are two, What is right? and What is good? Accepting this view, I shall give my own answers to his two questions.

First, then, how are we to tell what it is right to do, or what we ought to do, which, certain refinements apart, is the same question. There are two quite different streams of thought on this matter, and if we cared to ascend either one, it would take us back more than two thousand years. The two streams are legalism and teleology. The Pharisees were legalists who held that right conduct lay in conformity to divine law. The Stoics were legalists who held that the good life lay in conforming to natural law. Kant was a legalist who held that right conduct lay in conforming the principle of one's conduct to the law of non-contradiction. Ross is a legalist who holds that there are certain rules of promise-keeping, truth-telling, and so on, which lay obligations on us which at times are even stronger than the claim of the greatest good.

On the other side are the teleologists, who hold that the test lies in consequences—the view of Socrates, for example, and Epicurus and Bentham and Mill and Rashdall and Moore. It is my rare good fortune to have had Ross, Prichard and Carritt as teachers on the one side of this issue, and Rashdall and Moore on the other, and indeed to have had Moore as a guest for six months during the last war. I recall that one day at lunch I ventured to repeat to him some of Ross's objections to a teleological ethics. Moore's slow and quiet reply was: "It still seems to me self-evident that we always ought so to act as to produce the greatest good, that is, to make the world as much better as we can." That is the supreme maxim of the teleologists, the categorical imperative that they believe holds without exception: So act as to produce the greatest good. Here I follow them. On the actual consequences of our acts depends their objective rightness. On the intended consequences depends their subjective rightness.

When this test of rightness is proposed, there is one difficulty that is almost sure to be urged. It is that sometimes it seems plainly our duty so to act as *not* to produce the greatest good. Suppose you go into Macy's in New York in search of a fountain pen. The attendant has a lot of pens laid out on the counter, and is engrossed with another customer. You see a fine pen of just the kind you want, though it is more expensive than you can well afford. You reflect. Nothing would be easier than to slip that pen into your pocket unobserved and saunter out. That massive firm of Macy's would not tremble; it might never miss the pen, and if it did, would not toss on its pillow over it, while you would get real delight from your new possession. Is it not clear that your gain would be greater than Macy's loss, and therefore that you would be achieving the greater net good by walking out the door with a smile of satisfaction over your new prize, your expert light-fingeredness, and your ethical originality?

With one who argued in that way we should hardly know how to deal, and would probably much prefer to have him dealt with by a floorwalker or a magistrate. Still the thief has a point, and an extremely awkward one for the traditional ethics of consequences. Take his act of thievery in isolation, assume him to be secretive about his act and to suffer no pangs of conscience about it, assume Macy's to be careless enough not to discover the loss, and I am afraid that, single-handed, that thief can put Bentham, Mill, Sidgwick and Moore to rout. They all say, "So act as to produce the greatest good," to which he answers, with some plausibility, "That is exactly what I have done."

Of course, these great moralists would not approve such conduct, but their *theory* seems to do so, and we can only say to them: "We know that such conduct is wrong, and if your theory leads to its justification, so much the worse for the theory." But then if the wrongness does not depend on

11

the consequences, what does it depend on? Many moralists have been tempted to say, as Kant did, that it lies in the character of the act itself; stealing *as such* is wrong. But a little reflection shows that that too will not do. For if stealing as such is wrong, it is always wrong; and sometimes it clearly is not. The FBI man who abstracts a gun from the room of a murderous escaped convict is taking someone else's property, but we all agree that he is acting rightly, not wrongly, in doing so. And if asked why we say so, we should undoubtedly appeal to consequences.

I think this appeal is inescapable. But when we justify an act by its consequences, what consequences are we appealing to? It is not the consequences of this particular act, for they would sometimes justify what was wrong, as we have seen. Is it, then, the consequences of the rule of the act, in the sense of what would follow from everyone's adopting this rule? No, for that would require us to condemn much that is innocent. If everyone became a philosopher, the world's work would not get done; but does it follow that I am wicked in trying to be a philosopher? I certainly hope not. What is it, then, whose consequences settle the rightness or wrongness of an act, if it is neither the act itself nor the rule governing it?

There is perhaps no harder question in ethics. The answer I venture to give is close to Plato's and among contemporaries, to H. W. B. Joseph's. The consequences are those involved by *the pattern of life to which the act belongs.* That is vague, but not unmeaning. One can see on reflection that respect for property is bound up with one pattern of life, and stealing with another; and that one cannot fairly tear either out of that pattern and consider it out of the context. If stealing is right, so is deception, which is normally a part of it; so is the destruction of confidence; so is the disregard of other people's feelings, hopes and desires. These further practices are in principle bound up with it, and one cannot justify stealing without committing oneself to these too. What one must ask, therefore, is whether one is prepared to accept, not the single act, but the pattern of action, the network of practice, to which this act belongs. The plain man feels these implications, even if he has never explicitly traced them; that is why he is inclined, if you ask him why stealing is wrong, to say simply: "Why, if this is right, practically anything would be right; the bottom would fall out of morality." Respect for what others have is right because it is an integral part of a form of life that, as a whole, is good; stealing is wrong because the way of life implied in it would be a human disaster. And the plain man would feel, instinctively but soundly, that stealing a pen and taking the weapon of a dangerous criminal, though both could be called theft, belong to wholly different patterns of living.

This is my answer, such as it is, to the first question of ethics. That act—or more precisely, the network of practices involved in it—is right which would produce the greatest good.

I come now to the second question of ethics. Granting that an action is right when the pattern of conduct to which it belongs is productive of most good, the question at once arises, What makes anything good?

The answer I propose is as follows: there are three conditions of anything's being good, a general one and two special ones. The general one is that whatever is good is experience, or if you prefer, consciousness. In a world without consciousness, there would be nothing good. Suppose we were all to die tonight; would the Fifth Symphony have any value tomorrow, or the Taj Mahal, or *King Lear*, or the Mona Lisa? I think not. They would have potential value in the sense that causes would still be there which, if they acted on human minds, might produce experiences of value; but physical things have no value in themselves. When we ascribe goodness or value to *King Lear* as a work of art, we do not mean that certain marks on paper are good; we mean that the thoughts and feelings, the delight, the sympathy, the understanding gained by the reader or hearer are intrinsically good. Without these the value would vanish. What would be the importance of marks on paper, or of an extra mountain on the moon, or even of an extra galaxy or two, in a dead world?

Now for the two special conditions. Granted that experiences only are good, what makes them good, that is, intrinsically good, not good as means merely? Two things. First, they must fulfill some impulse of human nature. By an impulse I mean a drive, an appetite, an urge, a want, innate or acquired—the sort of demand that, when it rises to awareness of its end, is a desire. No earthworm of my acquaintance has shown any discernible passion for knowledge; my poodle does have a mild curiosity regarding the outside, though not the inside, of my philosophy books; his master has a pathetically genuine desire to understand what is in them. Where there is an appetite for knowledge, its fulfillment is felt as good; where there is not, knowledge is ashes in the mouth. The same is true of aesthetic interest. There are persons who, as tone-deaf, do not know what music means and therefore cannot love it; to them classical music, as Mark Twain would say, is as bad as it sounds. To a nature with no capacity for, and no impulse toward, friendship or religion or play or adventure, these things would have no value, for there would be nothing in such a nature which could respond to them, and find fulfillment or enrichment in them. Where they do fulfill, they are good.

It may be said that there are impulses whose fulfillment is evil. This is true in the sense that there are many that should not be indulged, like hatred or jealousy, for example. But why should they not? Because they are impulses whose indulgence thwarts and frustrates the other impulses both of ourselves and of those around us. To say that human nature is basically evil, as some theologians are nowadays saying, seems to me libelous. It is nearer the truth to say that it is fundamentally good, since in its realization all good lies. But an unrealized potency is neither good nor evil. Whether a given impulse shall be reined in or released depends on which would contribute more to human fulfillment as a whole, our own and others.

The second special condition is pleasure. I hark back to Aristotle in thinking that pleasure, or as I would rather say, satisfaction, normally accompanies fulfillment, and that if deprived of this accompaniment, fulfillment itself would be without value. Michelangelo is alleged to have said, indeed, in his hypochondriac way, that he worked only to get money to support his needy relatives, and Goethe that he had not had a week of happiness in his life. Both remarks are incredible. They are like saying that Willie Mays is miserable when playing baseball, or Van Cliburn in playing the piano. The successful employment of one's powers is the very prescription for happiness. To be sure, in some abnormal cases the capacity for pleasure is lost, but then the value of knowledge for the scholar and of art for the artist goes with it; the pitcher lies broken at the fountain. The thought of Newton or Einstein would of course still have its instrumental value for good or ill, no matter how they felt about it, but if they could not feel about it at all, if there was no fascination for them in discovery, no delight in following an argument, no more satisfaction in the play of ideas than in snoring in bed, then the life of the mind itself would have become a desert for them.

Well, there is my ethical theory, such as it is, in a nutshell. Its rule of conduct is, Choose that action or pattern of action which would produce the greatest good, meaning by "good" experiences that are fulfilling and satisfying. This is a naturalist ethics, based on human nature. It conceives of each man as a bundle of impulses seeking fulfillment, and the major goods of life as corresponding to these impulses. It conceives of the human race as an "unweeded garden" in which flowers and weeds of every variety are struggling to bring to bloom what is potential within them, the sunflower in an aspiring way, the violet in a more modest way, the crabgrass in so destructive a way that it must be held in check if it is not to choke the others. Morality is the gardener. It tills and waters and weeds its sprawling collection in the hope of a maximum crop of human good.

You will note that this sort of ethics has certain strong affinities. It is utilitarian but it is not hedonist, for it does not take happiness as the whole and sole good. It prizes self-realization, but not exclusively, because happiness also is essential. It is close to Dewey, but without his suspicion of intrinsic goods. It is close to Moore, though instead of holding that good is indefinable and non-natural, it takes it as both definable and natural. It is subjectivist because it makes all values relative to experience, but it is objectivist about moral judgment. The statement that Chamberlain did wrong at Munich is as objectively true or false as anything in chemistry, whether we ever discover the truth about it or not.

Now we come to the third issue we set out to deal with. If all political questions are in the end ethical questions, and the ethics one adopts is the kind I have outlined, how will it affect one's convictions in politics?

One's convictions in politics may move on two levels, one of general principle, the other of particular cases. Let us look first at the level of principle. I suppose what is basic in one's political convictions is one's belief about the ultimate ground of political rights and duties. The government now claims the right to take away from us a substantial part of our earnings and spend it in ways approved by itself, a right that was regarded, when put forward by Woodrow Wilson in 1913, as almost impossibly socialistic. Can that right be justified? Try to justify it, and you find yourself carried on to the ultimate question, By what right does the state itself exist and claim any rights over us at all? That question turns out, as one thinks about it, to be the same as, Why should I do what the state says? One of the pleasant things about political thinking, by the way, is how often you find yourself bringing down two cocoanuts with one stone. Whenever you explain a right, you also explain a duty, for a duty is the other end of a right; my right to have a book returned by you is the same thing, looked at from your end, as your duty to return the book to me. To explain the right of the state to order us about is to explain at the same time our duty to obey its laws. Very well, what is the ground of this right and duty?

With the kind of ethics at our disposal, that question will not cause us much trouble. Imagine the following dialogue between you and the state.

> YOU: *Why*, Mr. Johnson, should you tax my nerves, my honesty and my pocket every March in your yearly drive for a hundred billion dollars?
>
> THE STATE: Do you want communism to take over in South America and South Viet Nam?
>
> YOU: No, but what has this to do with . . . ?
>
> THE STATE: Just a moment; do you need better roads in Kansas?
>
> YOU: Yes, but—
>
> THE STATE: Do you want security for old people, care for veterans, jobs for the unemployed, post-offices, courts, policemen to protect you, uncensored newspapers, freedom to speak your mind, freedom to choose your own wife and church and business, the chance to educate your children . . . ?
>
> YOU: Yes, yes, of course I do, but—
>
> THE STATE: Is there anyone or anything but the state that could get these things for you?
>
> YOU: No, I suppose not.
>
> THE STATE: Could it get these things without the support of you and others like you?
>
> YOU: No doubt it couldn't.
>
> THE STATE: Well, would you rather have these things and pay your tax, or do without them and save your tax?
>
> YOU: Well, if you put it that way, there isn't much of a choice, is there?
>
> THE STATE: No; I thought you looked rather sensible. Now your check, please. It will be only a few hundred more than it was last year.

That bit of dialogue puts with brutal brevity the ground of political rights and duties. For all its power and dignity, a government is merely a means to an end, namely the good of the people served by it; and its claims on us arise from the fact that it is the *only* means to ends that we all want. We cannot deny its claims without disavowing either the value of these ends, which would be absurd, or its effectiveness as a means, and then the obvious course is not to get rid of it, but to improve it. Every government can be improved; none is sacrosanct, not even democracy; the best we can say of democracy is what Mr. Churchill said of it, that it is "the worst form of government except all those other forms that have been tried from time to time."

This is the true apology for any state, and all rights and duties must in the end be defended in the same way. If you are my landlord and I refuse to pay my rent, what argument would you present to me assuming, as is then perhaps unlikely, that I am capable of argument? You might say, "I surely have the right to payment for the use of my own property." But suppose I reply, "Where did you get any such right? I prefer to stay and not to pay." You plead, "But you promised to pay." To which I reply, "Why should I keep my promise if I'd rather not?" The psychological move at this point is no doubt to sputter; the logical move is to say "If you have the right to do this, you must in consistency grant it to others; and would you really prefer a society in which people broke promises and contracts at will?" If I am candid, I can only say No; and to be consistent with that answer, I shall have to concede both your right and my obligation. My doing so is the means to an end that I too want above all things.

Every government, every political right and duty, is thus a means to the ethical end, and must be justified by its relation to that end.

If this view is accepted, it eliminates at once a variety of theories that are popularly held. One is that our state is founded on religion. Our Bill of Rights is based on respect for the individual, regardless of race or class, and this respect is made possible, we are often told, only by the assurance—an assurance that is religious—that each man is an immortal soul of equal value in the eyes of his Maker. Now I am not criticizing religious belief, and I agree that a religious person has special reasons for valuing persons and their rights, but to say that this is the only basis for such regard is to imply that a man without religious convictions lacks any sufficient basis for recognizing—let us say—the rights of women or children, of Negroes or Puerto Ricans. This appears to be untrue. The reason for recognizing the claim of a colored boy or girl is not that it is endorsed by theological doctrine, but that this person has a potentiality for good that ought not to be repressed; and this potentiality is a fact that is there to be recognized by persons of all religions or none. The appeal to theology will not be decisive unless it is also an appeal to fact. It was once believed that a monarch could hold his throne only by the divine right of kings, that if a government were to have authority, church and state must be united, that an oath to tell the truth would not be binding unless made by a religious believer. These views rest on the conviction that the ultimate ground for duty is the will of God, and this conviction is questionable. It is questionable, first, because it implies, regarding Deity, that he does what he does, not because it is right, but because he wants to, which imputes to him a character below our own; and secondly, because it implies that if he willed that we should commit murder, that would make it right, which seems clearly untrue. The moral law is an immutable and objective law, which holds because the good is really good and the bad, bad; and only a morality so based is safe. The person who accepts it because it is the will of God will all too naturally conclude, if he loses his belief, that he has lost all reason for morality also. That is an illusion. Duty is no hound of Heaven, but so long as we believe in a genuine good and evil, we shall still find it pursuing us "down the arches of the years."

There is another traditionally popular view of the ground of rights that our theory must dismiss, a view proposed in no less a document than the Declaration of Independence. It is there laid down that men were endowed at their creation with "unalienable rights," and that among these are equality, life, liberty, and the pursuit of happiness. These are supposed to be "natural rights," belonging to us self-evidently as rational beings. They are not conferred by the state; they cannot be taken away by law; and since they belong to human nature as such, they precede the state and outlast it. No power can abridge them; no circumstances can qualify them. This doctrine has done noble service on behalf of oppressed people of all kinds; and oddly enough, though it was used first by those on the left to defend serfs against their exploiters, it is now being used by the right to defend capitalists against exploitation by the state.

Do we have these "natural rights"? In a sense we do. But this sense does not seem on reflection to be the sense of the Declaration. If the rights of life and liberty are self-evident ones that belong to each man simply in virtue of his rational nature, then they belong to him everywhere and always, as the properties of a triangle belong to it, as Kant thought the wrongness of stealing belonged to it. But do they? If an FBI man had observed Lee Harvey Oswald with his gun trained on the President, would he have violated a right to life on Oswald's part if he had fired first? Most reflective persons would not say so; they would say that even the right to life is "alienable" and may be forfeited. Is the right to freedom of speech an absolute right? Justice Black, who has a noble record of supporting freedom, says that under the first amendment it is; he thinks that a man should not be prosecuted for defamation of character, for the dissemination of obscenity, or even for falsely shouting "Fire!" in a theatre; if action is taken against this last man, says Black, it should be "not because of what he shouted but because he shouted." But here Mr. Black is, I believe, in a minority of one in the Supreme Court. Most others, inside and outside the Court, would hold that a man has no right, constitutional or natural, to put about malicious falsehoods or start a panic with a false report. The right to freedom, like the right to life, is limited. What imposes the limit? The same authority that confers the right, namely the public good. Just as a right is a means to the good, so when misuses of that means endanger the good, they may themselves be vetoed. Our theory that not only right but rights are derivative from the general good thus explains why we have some rights and do not have others. If I meet a Chinaman in a Pacific jungle, he and I may be beyond the jurisdiction of any state or court, but he has a right to decent treatment from me, based on the fact that he is a human being with powers and needs. These are natural rights. But he has no right to kill or enslave me, for such rights would be means to evil, not good. The only unqualified natural right is the right to consideration, that is, the right to have one's interests taken into account and regarded as of equal importance with the like good of others.

Our ethical theory does make a difference, then, to the principles of our politics; it supplies them an ultimate ground. If it does this, it is bound to affect our thinking about particular cases too. Take any of the measures that are being introduced under the broad head of social welfare by the present administration. Without brashly taking sides on these, one may point out what sort of argument would be relevant to them. The redemption of Appalachia, Medicare, price supports for farm products, a few hundred millions for new schools and scholarships, the reduction of excise taxes, the Peace Corps, all the measures for conservation, from the saving of eroding soil to saving the beauty of our highways—must they not all be defended or criticized in the same way, by taking them as more or less efficacious means to ends? Show that the spending of a certain sum would do more to promote the general good, in our specific sense of making possible a fuller realization of human faculty, than not expending it, or than expending it in other directions, and your case will be as conclusive as it can be.

It is an advantage of this way of thinking that it forces us to consider what can and cannot be done by law. If human good consists in the fulfillment of faculty, it is not something that can be handed out and passed around like spinach to waiting Popeyes. It must be achieved by individual effort. The chief business of government, as Bosanquet said, is not to produce the good life directly, but to hinder the hindrances to the good life. A gift of the Encyclopaedia Britannica to a moronic illiterate is not a gift at all, for there is nothing in it that he can make his own. Perhaps the profoundest difference between Mr. Goldwater and his opponents in the last election concerned this question of how much one can do by legislation. I think Mr. Goldwater was inclined to say that if some people are sunk in poverty and ignorance, it is because they lack the vital spark or drive that would lift them out of it and that nothing you could hand out to them would replace this. The liberals who opposed him would not dissent on this point, but they would raise a further question: Is the lack of drive something that belongs to these people by nature, or is it something produced in them by discouraging conditions which can themselves be altered? No doubt there are people of both kinds, and the problem is to know which is which. The problem of Appalachia confronts us again in the problem of foreign aid. It is hopeless to pour food and drink into the bottomless maw of the world's hunger if that maw is only made more insatiable by feeding it. The aim of such gifts is to enable the receivers to put their own house in order and to render continuing aid unnecessary. Clearly the Jack-in-the-box theory of the liberal is the more hopeful one, for it takes the view that most people do have the vital spring, but that it is being held down by material pressure and will leap up of its own accord when that pressure is removed. The magnificent success of the Marshall Plan suggests that, in Europe at least, the liberal theory is true, and its supporters stick to the faith that it will prove true also in Africa and South America.

Professionally the rationalist has little use for faith. Faith goes beyond the evidence, and that seems to him hardly moral. Reason in the form of induction tells him the consequence of his conduct; reason in the form of *a priori* insight enables him to appraise those consequences. He does not draw back from saying that such insight may rise to certainty. If, recalling an experience last night of reading a fine poem, and then an experience last year of an emergency operation without an anesthetic, he is asked which was more worth having, he does not grope about for an answer. And if you say to him, "Do you mean that no one, contemplating these two experiences, ever could reverse this order of value?" he answers, "Precisely, and if this is absolutism, make the most of it." He would regard relativism in such a case as confusion or moral sickness.

But in practice even the rationalist must appeal to faith. It is one thing to believe that to all human controversies there is a rational solution waiting to be found; it is much harder to believe that men will allow themselves to find it. "The love of truth," said A. E. Housman, "is the faintest of human passions"; and I am afraid that anyone who takes his cue from history, which Gibbon called "a register of the crimes, follies and misfortunes of mankind," will doubt whether men are, or can be, reasonable. Yet what distinguishes the rationalist is more than a conviction that reason has the right of way over cupidity and hatred, envy, anger and fear; it is also a peculiar faith, the faith that reason is present and the same in all men, and that, given a chance to hear its voice, men will listen to it and be ashamed not to heed it. They may use that chance, as they often have, to their own destruction. There is no way of proving that democracy will succeed. It is an adventure in optimism, a glorious gamble, an expression of indemonstrable faith that given their freedom men will use that freedom reasonably. In spite of the necklace of millstones that history has placed about his neck, that remains the hope and faith of the rationalist in politics.

LOVE AND JUSTICE

Robert O. Johann, S.J.

ROBERT O. JOHANN, S.J., is Adjunct Professor of Christian
Ethics at Fordham University. He has also taught at Loyola
University in Chicago and at Yale University. He is Council-
lor of the Metaphysical Society of America. He has contributed to several anthologies as well as to philosophical and
popular journals, and he is the author of *The Meaning of
Love* (1955).

The theme proposed for this essay is as urgent as it is broad.
Dissatisfaction with present performance in both its suggested areas is deep and widespread. Patterns and institutions which up to now were accepted as embodiments of love
and justice are increasingly denounced as betraying them.
Hence the vast and popular effort, cutting across every level
of society, to rethink the implications of these ideals for today's world and to forge, whatever the cost, new institutions
and procedures more in accord with their demands.

PROBLEM AND METHOD

The importance, however, of this effort is matched by its
difficulty. Something of the problem was manifested recently at a conference on the "Bad Samaritan" held at the
University of Chicago Law School. The conference grew out
of the shock provoked by the fatal stabbing in New York
last year of Catherine Genovese, whose cries for help went
unheeded by thirty-eight neighbors, and by a series of similar

instances since. It examined the problem of what to do with people who ignore other people dying in subways and on the street, and sought to lay the foundation for a body of legal theory to encourage the "Good Samaritan."

But as the New York *Times* (April 10, 1965) noted, there were not a few dissenting voices. They questioned whether or not it is possible to legislate charity, altruism, and physical or moral courage. That the majority of Americans would consider helping the neighbor in such circumstances a matter of charity rather than justice was borne out by the fact that seventy-five per cent of those questioned were opposed to legal punishment for the "Bad Samaritan." And yet that is the whole point. Is help in such situations something that is strictly owed, or is it rather a work of supererogation? Simone Weil, for example, began an essay on "Human Personality" as follows: " 'You do not interest me.' No man can say these words to another without committing a cruelty and offending against justice."[1] For this philosopher back in 1943, as for an increasing number today, a positive concern for one's neighbor is something that is strictly due. To be indifferent is more than to be unloving. It is to be unjust.

Part of the difficulty, of course, in understanding the relationship between love and justice stems from the confusion surrounding each of these terms even when taken separately. Take the case of love. Who would presume to tell us unequivocally what it means? A couple of years ago when C. S. Lewis wanted to write a book about love, it came out as a book about four loves. Indeed, in addition to the four types of love which he distinguished and to which he devoted separate sections of his work—namely: affection, friendship, sexual love and religious love or *agape*—Lewis also managed to discern three other types of love in which each of the preceding four were said to participate. Here we have "need love," "gift love," and a third kind which Lewis described as

[1] Simone Weil, *Selected Essays, 1934–43*, Richard Rees, trans. (London, 1962), p. 9.

"appreciative love."[2] Paul Tillich, writing about love, does much the same thing. He too has four categories or, as he prefers to call them, "four qualifications of love": *libido* (love as desire), *philia* (friendship), *eros* (the drive towards beauty and value), and finally once again *agape* (the religious dimension of love). Nor is he, any more than Lewis, satisfied with a fourfold division but must introduce, in addition, three other aspects. These are: love as emotion, love as an ontological power, and love as an ethical principle.[3]

Yet if the language of love is confusing, the language of justice is equally so. As Professor Del Vecchio pointed out in his classic work on justice:

> Justice is sometimes taken to be synonymous with or equivalent to law, sometimes to be distinct from law and superior to it. Justice in one of its aspects is held to consist in *conformity with law*, but it is also asserted that *law must conform to justice*. What at one moment is taken as the standard whereby to judge what is just and unjust can in turn, in its manifestation as mere empirical fact, be itself judged in the same way; this happens when we appeal, in the name of justice, to a higher ideal criterion which transcends all rules of positive law and must therefore rest on some other foundation.[4]

The contemporary and widespread practice of civil disobedience and the discussions which this practice has evoked in the press are obviously a case in point.

But if we distinguish the two senses of justice to which Del Vecchio refers as legal justice on the one hand, and ethical justice on the other, we are still not done with the matter. For ethical justice, this "higher" justice, is itself open to a whole range of interpretations. Indeed, the thrust of Del Vecchio's work is precisely to trace the development of ethi-

[2] C. S. Lewis, *The Four Loves* (London, 1960).

[3] Paul Tillich, *Love, Power, and Justice* (London, 1954).

[4] Giorgio Del Vecchio, *Justice; An Historical and Philosophical Essay*, A. H. Campbell, ed. (Edinburgh, 1952), p. 1.

cal justice from its status as a universal and comprehensive virtue, such as Plato considered it to be, to its modern status as a distinct virtue alongside others. This latter is justice in the proper or juridical sense, a matter of rights and obligations. Nor are the distinctions over at this point. Following Aristotle, juridical justice is still divided into distributive justice and retributive justice, and the dispute continues as to which is primary. Some authors, for example, give the primacy to retributive justice and then proceed to divide it into equalizing (or commutative) justice, and corrective (or penal) justice. Others, like Del Vecchio himself, give distributive justice the first place, but then subdivide this into recognitive justice and attributive justice.[5]

We could go on. Enough, however, has been said to indicate that the concepts of love and justice, even when taken separately, are anything but unambiguous. We should not be surprised, therefore, if there is hardly less confusion when we compare them to one another. At first glance the terms love and justice suggest completely different things, and evoke completely different responses. Love we think of as something spontaneous, justice as something deliberate. Love is something felt; justice something owed. Justice is cold, but love is warm. There is something external about the juridical relation. Its terms are kept separate, distinct; their independence is emphasized. Love on the other hand is a matter of union. Love is liberal, generous, magnanimous. Justice is calculating. Justice is something objective and public. Love seems more subjective and seeks privacy.

Yet, for all this, the two terms have a tendency to move towards one another and to overlap. We have already referred to the universal conception of justice. At this stage in man's reflection, justice is the supreme value and charity or love is one of its subdivisions. On the other hand, under the Christian influence, philosophers have not been lacking who have made love supreme and seen justice as a kind of

[5] For a discussion of this question, see Del Vecchio's chapter on the "Logical Elements of Justice" (*op. cit.*, pp. 83–90).

minimal realization of love. Again, if we think of the Great Commandment, the commandment to love, then love becomes a debt we owe and its payment a matter of justice. Conversely, Leibniz defines justice itself as love; the "love of the wise man," he calls it.[6] And even Del Vecchio, for all his insistence on justice as a distinct virtue, cannot help noting that justice "is the overcoming of individuality, the projection of the *ego* in the form of the *alter* . . ."[7]—all of which makes justice sound very much like love.

The problem confronting us, therefore, is one of extraordinary complexity. Indeed, the long history of the concepts of love and justice has involved them in such a tangle that any attempt to unravel them directly, at least in the time allotted us here, would be hopeless. What I propose to do, then, is to tackle the problem indirectly. Instead of wrestling at first with either notion by itself, or with both of them together, I suggest that our best course at the outset, however perverse the suggestion may sound, is to introduce a third notion, that, namely, of *creative responsibility*. In the light of an analysis of man's vocation to a life of creative responsibility, I think something significant can be said about both the distinction and inter-relatedness of our two concepts —love and justice.

CREATIVE RESPONSIBILITY

The notion of responsibility has its roots in that objective awareness which is characteristic of man. In his book, *Man's Place in Nature*, Max Scheler distinguishes man from the lower animals precisely in terms of this capacity for objectivity. Unlike man, the brute animal "lives, as it were, ecstati-

[6] "Justitiam igitur . . . commodissime ni fallor definiemus *caritatem* sapientis, hoc est sequentem sapientiae dictata" (*Die philosophischen Schriften von G. W. Leibniz*, C. I. Gerhardt, ed. [7 vols., Berlin, 1875–90], III, p. 386).

[7] Del Vecchio, *op. cit.*, p. 158.

cally immersed in its environment which it carries along as a snail carries its shell. It cannot transform the environment into an object."[8] The animal's actions are all reactions to stimuli as here and now affecting the present condition of the organism. For the animal, the environment does not exist in itself as objective or in its otherness but only as impinging subjectively on its psychophysical structure. With man, however, all this is changed. Man is precisely the being who has emerged or detached himself from the determinisms of nature and holds the disposition of his life in his own hands. For man, the environment begins to exist on its own terms. It becomes a world acting upon man and calling for his personal answer. This answer is not automatic. It is something that man himself can shape and mold. His intellectual awareness enables man to appreciate the objective values and factors inherent in a situation and to shape his action to meet them.

The basic notion of objectivity thus leads us to the idea of responsibility. For since objectivity puts us in the presence of the other as other, it makes our life fundamentally a matter of encounter and interaction. It is less a business of setting up particular goals for ourselves or of conforming to determinate patterns and laws than it is of responding to actions upon us. Moreover, our response to the actions of others proceeds in the light of our understanding of them. This understanding or interpretation of what is going on may be more or less adequate. It is indeed the business of thought to make the interpretation as adequate as possible. Thought by itself, however, is never sufficient. In addition to his habitual knowledge, a man must bring to each encounter a fundamental attitude of attention, a basic readiness to listen. If his response is to be adequate, it must be in terms of what is here and now being said to him.

In addition, however, to being reactions to interpreted actions upon us, our own actions as responsible must also be

[8] Max Scheler, *Man's Place in Nature,* Hans Meyerhoff, trans. (New York, 1961), p. 39.

made in anticipation of answers to our answers. As H. Richard Niebuhr remarks—and it is he who has done perhaps more than anyone else to develop this notion of responsibility thematically:

> An agent's action is like a statement in a dialogue. Such a statement not only seeks to meet, as it were, or to fit into, the previous statement to which it is an answer, but is made in anticipation of reply. It looks forward as well as backward; it anticipates objections, confirmations and corrections. It is made as part of a total conversation that leads forward and is to have meaning as a whole. . . . So considered, no action taken as an atomic unit is responsible. Responsibility lies in the agent who stays with his action, who accepts the consequences in the form of reactions and looks forward in a present deed to the continued interaction.[9]

This notion of continuity is important, for it implies the perduring identity of self in a continuing community of agents to which, indeed, response is being made. As Niebuhr points out: "There could be no responsible self in an interaction in which the reaction to one's response comes from a source wholly different from that whence the original action issued."[10] Responsibility, therefore, implies a kind of social continuity.

If, then, we bring all these elements together we have Niebuhr's definition of responsibility. It is, he says, "the idea of an agent's action as response to an action upon him in accordance with his interpretation of the latter action and with his expectation of response to his response; and all of this in a continuing community of agents."[11]

The definition is a good one, but it can be pushed farther. For we still have to ask: What is the ultimate context or horizon of man's responsibility? The answer is Being itself. To

[9] H. Richard Niebuhr, *The Responsible Self: An Essay in Christian Moral Philosophy* (New York, 1963), p. 64.
[10] *Ibid.*, p. 65.
[11] *Ibid.*

31

be responsible at all is to be infinitely so. Human responsibility is not delimited or confined to any particular order within the whole range of being. For to be responsive to the other as other is to be responsive to it precisely as existing in itself, precisely as being. Since beyond any particular being there are always others, no particular being can either exhaust or ground our capacity to respond to it. The value, therefore, whose presence to the self defines and constitutes its existence as a responsible agent is beyond all particularity. It is the absolute and all-encompassing value of Being itself, the ultimate ground in which everything that is participates. It is this correlativity and openness to Being itself that gives man his identity as a personal subject, as "I". And it is by being responsive to the exigencies of this value in all that he does, in all his encounters, that man achieves his integrity as a personal subject.

Niebuhr's notion of man as responder is thus akin to Heidegger's image of man as "Shepherd of Being." Any human response is implicitly an affirmation of Being itself. Man is by vocation Being's agent, the attendant of Being, called to promote its fuller presence in each situation in which he finds himself. Failure to live up to this vocation is not only to negate that value by whose presence he lives; it is also, at the same time and as a consequence, to betray his own identity as a person. It is thus that the ontology of the person implicit in the notion of responsibility leads us immediately into the realm of morality, the realm of right and wrong. And it is about this that I would now like to say a few words, since it is directly relevant to the overall theme of our paper.

The foundation of man's moral life is, as I see it, the dynamic relation of the human self to Absolute Being. By his very constitution as a self man is called upon absolutely to affirm Being in all his interactions. What this affirmation of Being requires, that is, what actually constitutes an adequate response to Being in any particular situation, is a matter for discerning intelligence. It will depend not only on the determinate facts of the situation, but just as importantly on the concrete possibilities which man's presence to Being opens up to him. Morality, therefore, is necessarily a matter of invention and creativity. It does not merely look backwards to patterns already achieved, but forward to their enhancement. The ultimate norm in the moral realm and its only absolute law is thus the law of intelligent responsiveness. To be moral is to be for Being, to live in its light, to seek always in all the situations in which we find ourselves to promote its reign. If we take reason as the faculty of the Absolute, then to be moral is to be reasonable in the fullest possible sense.

This is not to say that there are no other norms or precepts which can serve as guidelines in the making of a moral decision. For we are not related to the Absolute and Infinite except through the mediation of the relative and finite. Our vocation, therefore, to be responsive to Being, the absolute and all-inclusive value, is not one that can be fulfilled in a void. Our promotive response to Being must necessarily be embodied in our relationships to the things and people who surround us. In the person's relations to his complex environment, reason discerns certain types of comportment as generally consonant with his fundamental dynamism as Being's agent, and certain other types as generally dissonant with it. These values and disvalues can be articulated in propositions and systematized into general codes of behavior. They become part of a moral tradition which grows and develops from generation to generation and whose function is to educate and awaken the individual to the abiding claims of Absolute Being on his responsibility. As the requirements of intelligent responsiveness, these claims have objective validity. Their articulation and preservation in traditional codes, moreover, has the importance of making possible a cumulative growth of moral insight over the years. To deny their relevance would be to deny the continuity of human experience and history and all the wisdom laboriously acquired in the past.

For all their relevance, however, such codes cannot be finally decisive in our moral choices. For the context through which Being itself makes its claim upon us is a non-systematic one. It is a context full of conflicts and cross-purposes. Filtered through this context, the one overriding claim of Being breaks up into a variety of claims which are often at odds with one another and whose sum is never more than a kind of coincidental manifold. What is required, therefore, is a constant weighing of one value against another, and of one disvalue against another. What we must look to is the election of that course of action which in the light of all its foreseeable consequences is most consistent with our vocation to promote Being. What alone is morally decisive, therefore, is the total sense of an action as seen in the concrete situation to which it is a response, and as judged in the light of man's fundamental vocation as a person.

From this point of view we can see the fundamental insight in the Existentialist view of man as a *project* and in its consequent rejection of conventional Natural Law theory. For human nature, properly speaking, is not something complete and self-enclosed, a detailed map for guiding our conduct. Human nature is a task to be accomplished. It is reason itself as open to the Infinite and called to respond to it in, through, and beyond the finite. Correspondingly, reason's role is not something passive. Its function is not simply to record *what is* as the pattern to be followed, but in the light of Being to innovate new ways of behaving. Its vocation is not merely to register natural data but to judge and transform them. Instead of being true to nature, therefore, as something fixed and settled standing over against it, reason's task is to be true to itself or correlatively to the requirements of Being itself. Since the moral order is not grounded in determinate nature but in reason's openness to the Absolute, the morally right is not what conforms to determinate nature but what conforms to the dictates of a reason enlisted in Being's service. From this point of view, being moral means being reasonable and being reasonable means precisely acting in accord with reason's recommendations—a reason open to the Absolute and bent on fulfilling its claims.

In the light of this ontology of the person and its ethical implications, we are now in a position, I think, to say something significant about the nature of love and of justice, and about their relation to one another.

RESPONSIBILITY AND LOVE

The relationship of what has been said to the idea of love should be immediately apparent. We have rooted the idea of responsibility in man's openness to the Absolute, in the fact that at the very core of his being he is constituted as being-for-Being. This means that he can be true to himself only insofar as he lives out in all his dealings this fundamental relationship to transcendent value. He is, indeed, a project of universal love. If he seeks himself, for example, to the exclusion of others he contradicts himself. So also if he sets up some minor mutuality which is hostile to the interests of the larger community. Only in the measure that he freely and deliberately devotes himself to the enhancement and fulfillment of everything he encounters within the unity of universal fulfillment does he accomplish the task which his own nature as a person has set him.

To speak, however, about love in man's life as a task to be accomplished, as something to which he must deliberately devote himself, as indeed something that is owed, is to run into the difficulty that we mentioned earlier, the difficulty about commanding someone to love. It seems to collide head on with our experience of love as something spontaneous and felt, an attraction which we undergo rather than a course which we ourselves choose. It seems to intellectualize love too much, to make it too much a matter of head and not enough of heart. In this it runs up against the admonition which Charles Peirce gave in this area, one which I think would be endorsed by most people instinctively: "In regard to the greatest affairs of life," he wrote, "the wise man follows his heart and does not trust his head. This should be the method of every man, no matter how powerful his intellect."[12] In order to resolve this apparent conflict and throw further light on what we mean by love as a task, we shall have to say a few words about the relative roles of head and heart in our pursuit of values. More particularly, we shall have to say something about our experience of the good as a matter of fact, and our quest for the good as a matter of freedom.

The good is not immediately the term of thought but of feeling and sensibility. It is not disclosed by a process of dispassionate inquiry but only through the stresses and strains of personal involvement. The good is what we lack when we are sad, and have when we are glad. It causes us worry when it is threatened, outrage when it is violated, grief when it fades and disappears. The good is what is experienced as congenial, healing, fulfilling, worth fighting and struggling for. It never comes merely as the answer to a question. It is always the answer to a prayer. The role of the heart in disclosing the good is thus undeniable. If we did not experience our own being in terms of desires and aspirations we would never be aware of anything at all as good.

Granting, however, that the heart thus lights up the realm of value, we must still ask whether its promptings by themselves are reliable guides. Are "reasons of the heart" reasons enough for what we do? To think of the pathetic, often destructive choices they have been called on to justify is already to begin to doubt it. The difficulty with following the heart is that it leads in different directions at the same time. Although it illumines the whole range of values, it does so indiscriminately. If by *heart* we mean the dynamic structure of man, his affective accord with all that is naturally congenial, then we must say that the heart is a bundle of distinct and often conflicting drives. Some urge a man toward

[12] *Collected Papers of Charles Sanders Peirce*, Charles Hartshorne, Paul Weiss, and Arthur Burks, eds. (8 vols., Cambridge, 1931–58), 1.653.

whatever is necessary for his well-being as an individual organism. Others on a deeper level compel him to look for his completion and a deepening of self-awareness through association and union with his fellows. Most profound, however, and completely transforming these prior dynamisms, is that affective kinship with Being itself which we have described as constituting man's nature as a person and which calls him continually to live in its light and be bent on promoting its reign.

The realm of goods lighted up by man's inclinations is thus all but chaotic in its diversity. The ease and comfort of material abundance, the security of social acceptance, the gracious support of friendship, the healing intimacy of conjugal love, the delight in order and rationality, the exhilaration of creativity, the abiding consolation of being in the service of Being—all these are terms of the heart's hankerings. With respect to our feeling their attractive force we are not free. But the point we would make is that unless they are sorted out and freely integrated in a total quest, their separate tuggings can tear the heart apart.

What is needed, therefore, is first a work of intelligent discernment. Man's manifold aims must be distinguished from one another and then grasped in their interconnectedness. A kind of hierarchy must be established on the basis of objective importance. What counts here is not the mere force of feeling but how it is interpreted; not the brute tug of a particular good but the meaning it has for our total life. For example, a man might make any of the particular goods that we have indicated a center of his attention and the focus of his life-quest. But if in the process he goes counter to the claims of Being itself on his life, then he will become divided and alienated from himself as a person. In theological terms, he gains the whole world but still loses his soul, and this not in some afterlife but here and now. For if a responsive relation to Being itself is what constitutes our identity and integrity as persons, then it is clear that a life in accord with this relationship conditions the full and adequate enjoyment of any other good.

But such an ordering of our lives in the service of Being can only be accomplished freely. In animals the ordering of drives is instinctive. With man, only persistent reflection combined with determined docility to its findings can bring it about.

This brings up a further point. For docility to the findings of intellect means keeping them steadily in view. Besides discernment, therefore, there is a need for constant recollection. For the heat of action tends to distract us from everything except the immediate goal. We become hypnotized by the particular, caught up in its vicissitudes and, with our attention thus monopolized, fluctuate between extremes of joy and sadness that are out of all proportion to their occasions. Recollection, on the other hand, enables us to bring all our separate strivings into the ultimate orbit of the person's relation to Being. As Jean Guitton observes, the recollected man is able to extract even from his troubles a mysterious increase of being, whereas the most intense pleasure, if it is not assumed by the spirit, leaves us restless and empty.[13] Failure to stand in the presence of Being corrupts everything. For those, however, who are mindful of it and bent on its service, even frustration can contribute to growth.

The intellect's final service to the heart is one of purifying criticism. The most dedicated person is still open to confusing his isolated interests with the cause of Being itself. Only unremitting self-criticism can ensure that our efforts to promote Being do not degenerate into flurries of self-seeking and that earnestly pursued reforms do not become forms of evasion. This remark about the need for self-criticism will have special relevance, too, in the next section when we take up the matter of justice and the question of what Locke called "the appeal to Heaven" against the established juridical order. As Del Vecchio notes, such an attack on the written laws "may be inspired by very different motives: by the purest aspiration to a more perfect justice or by the selfish desire to evade one's

[13] Cf. Jean Guitton, *Essay on Human Love* (New York, 1951).

duties. Criticism and in particular rigorous *self-criticism* is therefore necessary in this connection; too often the 'spirit of revolution' has misused the sacred name of justice to cover impure passions and one-sided interests."[14] But more about this later.

Enough, I think, has been said to show the distinction between love as an emotion and love as a task, and also the connection that exists between them. More especially it should be clear how love as an emotion or a felt attraction for some particular good is an insufficient guide for the total orientation of our lives. This is especially true in my relation to other persons. It sometimes comes about—and anyone who has ever been in love will know what I mean—that another person will appear to me as especially lovable. This is not something I choose. It is something that happens. Due to a variety of factors, including a certain complementarity on the psychophysical level, but above all because of a reciprocity of consciousness that develops between us, I find this other being for all his otherness as nonetheless somehow inclusive of me. My own good exists and is preserved in him. Loving such a person is not felt as a task but as a joy. It is not something I experience as owed; it is something I want to do.

But even here the element of task is not absent. For if our relationship is not to develop into what might be called an *égoïsme à deux*, an exclusive mutuality that is indifferent and even hostile to the interests and claims of the larger community in which we find ourselves, then we must see to it that this very relationship takes its place in the larger community. Unless you and I who feel an attraction for one another are lovingly responsive also to all those others for whom we feel no such attraction, whom we experience simply as others, as exclusive of ourselves, then our very love for one another will be corrupted at its root. By failing to live up to our vocation as persons, which as we have seen is a vocation to universal love, we will each of us become alien-

[14] Del Vecchio, *op. cit.*, p. 157.

ated from himself as a person and so alienated from the other.

What this means, therefore, is that our actions will be true to ourselves and to the requirements of all our relationships only if they are deliberately ordered in the direction of a universal love. The commandment to love universally is not something imposed on us from the outside; it is simply a formulation of the very exigencies of our beings as persons. It is the enunciation of a requirement flowing immediately from that openness to the Absolute which first of all constitutes us responsible persons.

RESPONSIBILITY AND JUSTICE

Just as our analysis of responsibility was able to throw light on the nature of love in human life, so also I think it will illuminate the nature and foundation of justice.

First of all it should be noted how the achievement of truly responsible action and the achievement of justice, taken as a universal and comprehensive virtue, practically coincide. For justice in this general sense is had when all our actions in whatever circumstances are such as they ought to be. It prescribes only in a general way that our actions correspond to the actual values and factors inherent in the situation in which they take place. But such correspondence is precisely what we mean by responsiveness. From this point of view, it is quite possible to speak about doing justice to other realities besides persons. Thus, for example, Tillich writes, "All things . . . so to speak, call on us with small or loud voices. They want us to listen, they want us to understand their intrinsic claims, their justice of being. They want justice from us."[15] And such justice would be denied if, for example, we should torture an animal capriciously or play a game of darts using a great masterpiece as a target. Our injustice in these instances would consist precisely in our irresponsibility. But

[15] Tillich, *op. cit.*, p. 84.

this is injustice only in the broad sense, since it is not here a question of withholding or taking away from another what strictly belongs to him. Since every reality below the level of person lacks self-possession, it is incapable of possessing anything else. It does not have anything as strictly its own, as belonging to it, and consequently cannot be deprived of the same.

We are thus brought to the notion of justice in the strict sense which can exist only between persons. As Del Vecchio remarks: "Justice is essentially social, . . . its true and proper manifestations are found only where the acts and the claims of several persons meet, and . . . its specific function is to establish between these their due limits and harmonious proportions."[16] But even here where justice is strictly a matter of rights and corresponding obligations, the notion of responsibility will be illuminating.

It is impossible to treat of justice in the strict sense without taking up the question of rights. Justice has to do with the rights of others. The first question we have to ask, then, is: How does a person come to have rights? What is the basis of human rights? For as Josef Pieper remarks, ". . . no obligation to do justice exists unless it has as its presupposition this idea of the due, the right, the *suum*."[17] And hence he must raise the question: "How does anything come to belong to a person, anyway? And how does it so truly belong to him that every man and every human authority has to grant it to him and allow him to keep it?"[18]

One way to approach this problem is to note, as Pieper does (following Thomas Aquinas), that " 'If the act of justice is to give to each man his due, then the act of justice is preceded by the act whereby something becomes his due.' "[19] From this point of view, "Justice is something that comes second:

[16] Del Vecchio, *op. cit.*, p. 42.
[17] Josef Pieper, *Justice*, L. E. Lynch, trans. (New York, 1955), p. 15.
[18] *Ibid.*, pp. 12–13.
[19] *Ibid.*, p. 13.

Right comes before justice. If something is due to a man as his own, the fact of its being due to him has not come into existence through justice."[20]

What then is the act by which something first of all becomes due to a man, and which is nevertheless not an act of justice? An immediate answer might be to indicate such acts as agreements, treaties, promises, legal decisions, and so forth. Such an answer, however, is not sufficient. For besides the fact that it would be completely unable to account for natural rights—my right to life, for example, which is not based on any positive action—it is also an insufficient ground for the notion of positive rights as well. What right do I have to the keeping of a promise, or the fulfilling of an agreement? The fact that rights flow from such things as agreements and promises presupposes a juridical order already established and is consequently unable to ground it. Thus it is that Pieper, still following Aquinas, turns to something more fundamental. Citing the Angelic Doctor he writes: " 'It is through creation that the created being first comes to have his rights.' By virtue of creation first arises the possibility of saying: 'Something is my due.' "[21]

Yet this answer is not enough either. For as Pieper himself notes, "stones, plants and animals have also been created, yet we cannot say that they have their due in the strict sense of the word."[22] As we ourselves remarked earlier, since a non-personal being does not possess itself, it cannot strictly be said to possess anything else. It cannot have anything belonging to it in the proper sense of the word. It is for this reason that Pieper is forced to look for the foundation of rights in the nature of the being who is said to have rights. His final position, therefore, is that man has rights because he is "a *Person*—a spiritual being, a whole unto himself, a being that exists for itself and of itself, that wills its own proper perfection. Therefore, and for *that very reason*, something *is* due to

[20] Josef Pieper, *op. cit.*, p. 13.
[21] *Ibid.*, p. 14.
[22] *Ibid.*, p. 15.

man in the fullest sense, *for that reason* he does inalienably have a *suum,* a 'right' which he can plead against everyone else, a right which imposes upon every one of his partners the obligation at least not to violate it."[23] In short, "Man has inalienable rights because he is created a person by the act of God."[24]

This is as far as Pieper goes in his investigation of the origin of human rights, and in stopping here he is in accordance with a long tradition of thinking on this subject. It is my opinion, however, that more still has to be said. For the fact that God has created me a person still does not give me any right except in the presence of other persons. I have no rights in the presence of impersonal nature. A tornado does not do an injustice if it deprives me of life. If I were the only person in the world it would not be the case that I *had* rights but no one around to respect them. I would not have rights at all. Other persons are not therefore required simply to do justice to rights already constituted. The presence of other persons is needed if we are going to speak of rights in the first place.

But we can go further. The personal other is not only a necessary condition for the fact that my existence takes on the character of a claim or right. It is also a sufficient condition. And here we get back to the notion of responsibility. It is because I am in your presence, you who are a person endowed with objective awareness and called by nature to respond to beings in terms of what they are and do, that the reality of my person and my action first takes on the character of a claim or right. It is because you as a person are obliged to respond to me as a person that I have a right to such a response, that you are wrong when you do not give it, and that I can urge that wrong against you. Right does indeed come before justice, but it does not come before the obligation to do justice, which is identical with your nature as a person. My right to be treated as a person is founded on your obligation to treat me as a person. Apart from this obligation,

23 *Ibid.,* p. 20.
24 *Ibid.,* p. 21.

which is to say, apart from you, I have no rights. The act, therefore, by which a person first of all acquires rights is not his creation as a person by God but rather his insertion as a person in a society of persons. Besides this nothing else is needed.

This may seem like a small point, but it has important consequences for one's whole approach to the question of justice. I shall conclude this section by enumerating just three of them.

First of all, the theory of the origin of rights which I have just outlined serves both to internalize injustice and at the same time to supply a more immediate foundation for the inalienability of rights. So much emphasis has been placed on the external nature of justice and injustice that the really essential and tragic consequences of the latter have been lost sight of. As should be clear from what we have already said, injustice is not done by the mere fact that my reality as a person is ignored or because something that belongs to me is taken away. For the whole of impersonal nature ignores my personhood and not infrequently by its inroads deprives me of what is mine. Injustice is done only because you who are obliged to be responsive to the personal character of my being and activity refuse to be so. The injustice is in you.

This is the profound truth behind the idea that something incomparably worse befalls him who does an injustice than happens to the one against whom the injustice is committed. You will recall the remark of Socrates: "My dear Callicles, to receive a box on the ears wrongfully is not the greatest of outrages, nor even to fall into the hands of a murderer or a pickpocket . . . To do such an injustice to another is a far greater evil for the doer of the injustice than it is for the victim."[25] Because you are obliged by your very nature as a person to be responsive to me, you corrupt yourself in your personhood when you refuse to be so. And hence, too, the inalienability of my rights. Since my rights are founded on

[25] Plato *Gorgias* 508.

your nature as a person, no action of yours which is posterior to that nature can deprive me of those rights. You may indeed refuse to treat me as a person, and in the process undo yourself. But you cannot take away my right so to be treated.

Secondly, the theory we have outlined supplies a positive content that is often lacking in treatments of justice. When, for example, my rights are explained as constituted independently of your obligations as a person towards me, then all you wind up owing me in justice is non-interference with my rights. You do not owe me help. You just owe me not to do harm to me or to correct the harm that you have done. Hence the opinion to which we referred earlier which does not see the "Bad Samaritan" as failing in justice but only as lacking charity. In such a view, I am not obliged to help you to get out of the ditch unless I was the one who pushed you into it. But this, I think, is mistaken. My obligation to be responsive to you not only forbids me to hurt you positively, it also forbids me to be indifferent to you, to comport myself in your presence as if you were not there, to pass you by as if you were some mere thing. When you, here before me, are in distress, I cannot be unconcerned or refuse you reasonable help without equivalently negating your existence as a person. By omitting the response I owe you, I wrong you. I withhold something which, by reason of my nature as a person, you have a right to expect from me, something which is your due. I therefore fail not merely in charity but in justice.

Finally, by founding the rights of persons not on something independent of their relationship to one another but precisely on their mutual obligations of responsiveness, the emphasis is put where it belongs in the pursuit of justice. For justice can never be attained so long as each person is solely preoccupied with what is due to *him*, with *his* rights, and not with what *he* himself *owes* to others. Such preoccupation is simply another form of egoism and, in place of justice and order, it leads only to perennial strife. It is completely lacking in that overcoming of individuality and that subordination of self to a trans-subjective standard which is, as Del Vecchio observes, at the very heart of justice.[26]

LOVE AND JUSTICE

Having thus rooted both love and justice in the ontological constitution of the person as open and responsive to Being, we are in a position now to indicate briefly and by way of conclusion their relationships to one another.

What should be immediately clear from all we have said, is the mutual interdependence of love and justice. There can be no love without justice, and no justice without love. Love without justice is mere sentimentality. Justice without love is at best a contentious legalism.

There is no love without justice. The reason for this is that my love is untrue to itself if it is not universal. I cannot live up to my vocation to be for Being unless my active concern for Being is deliberately extended to all its participations. To seek only myself apart from others, or to love some at the expense of others, is at the same time to betray Being and undo myself. But this intention to be for Being universally, to give the response I owe to all its participations even where I feel no attraction, even where the being in question is a stranger and alien to myself, where it is experienced precisely in its otherness, this intention is none other than the deliberate intention to do justice.

On the other hand, there is no justice without love. For as we have seen, the very foundation of justice is that affective kinship with Being, that affinity of myself with Being itself, that first of all constitutes me a person and makes of my life a project of love. Only insofar as I deliberately set out to live up to that love in all my encounters, even with strangers, will justice be done. Only in the light of my love for Being will I be able to affirm the other in his otherness and really let, as Heidegger says, the other fully be himself.

[26] Del Vecchio, *op. cit.,* p. 158.

Thus, if justice and love are mutually interdependent, it nonetheless remains true that love is the principle of justice. We may sum up their relationships, therefore, by saying with Tillich that justice is "the form in which and through which love performs its work."[27] Since love is at work in justice, indeed, since love is at stake in justice, a society can never rest content with the level of justice it has achieved. The sense and order of justice in a particular society represents, as Nédoncelle observes, only the present level of the work accomplished by love.[28] It maintains what love has achieved. But the love which is at its root is constantly pushing it forward. For besides being the origin of justice, love is also its consummation. Justice preserves and fosters the integrity and independence of persons who are ultimately called to communion. But the final meaning of love is the realization of that communion. What Aristotle said of justice, that neither the Evening Star nor the Morning Star is as glorious, could even more truly be said of love.

[27] Tillich, *op. cit.*, p. 71.
[28] Cf. Maurice Nédoncelle, *Vers une philosophie de l'amour et de la personne* (Paris, 1957), pp. 71–72.

RESPONSIBILITY AND FREEDOM[1]

Kurt Baier

KURT BAIER, now Professor and Chairman of the Department of Philosophy at the University of Pittsburgh, has also taught at the University of Melbourne, the Australian National University, the University of Illinois, and Cornell University. He is former President of the Australasian Association of Philosophy. He has contributed articles on ethics and social philosophy to American and British philosophical journals, and is the author of *The Moral Point of View* (1958).

The remarkable vigor of the freewill controversy is undoubtedly due to the far-reaching social implications which one of the standard positions in this controversy is supposed to have. For from that position a stinging attack can be launched on a deeply-entrenched institution, the practice of punishment, over whose justifiability conservatives and progressives are always ready to do battle anyway. The argument by which this is done (which I shall call the Argument from Determinism) starts from the undeniable advance of the sciences, infers that everything, including the will, is causally determined, and from that deduces the bondage of the will. On this basis it then erects the contentious conclusion that nobody is to

[1] Work on this paper was facilitated by a research grant from the Carnegie Corporation and IBM to the Department of Philosophy of the University of Pittsburgh for a philosophical investigation of a broad range of value problems. I have greatly profited from discussions with my colleagues and several visitors who came to Pittsburgh in connection with this research project, especially Professors A. G. N. Flew and David Braybrooke.

49

blame for anything and that consequently punishment is never deserved, hence never legitimate. Surprisingly, most of the serious work on this Argument relates to its first part, the question of whether or not the advance of the sciences shows that the will is unfree. Very little has been said to explain why the bondage of the will should render all punishment undeserved and so illegitimate. The discussion which comes closest to this latter question is that between hard and soft determinists.[2] But even here we mostly get only bald assertions. The soft determinists claim that determinism is perfectly compatible with the freedom of the will because determinism is perfectly compatible with a person's being able to do something other than what he is doing, or with his not being compelled to do it, or with his doing it of his own free will or some other similar condition. But nothing is said to show why having one or the other of these abilities or being in one of these conditions should be tantamount to the will's being free in a sense which is relevant to the justification of punishment. And the hard determinists assert, equally baldly, that determinism is not compatible with the freedom of the will because possessing these abilities is not sufficient to establish the freedom of the will. But nothing is said to show that the proof of our not having these abilities is sufficient to establish the unjustifiability of punishment. Thus, these arguments about the incompatibility of determinism with the freedom of the will may well succeed in demonstrating their startling conclusions in some sense of "freedom of the will." However, such a demonstration is not sufficient to solve the problem which has continued to exercise philosophers. To that end, it is necessary, in addition, to show that the sense of "free will" for which the demonstration was given is a relevant sense and the only one that is relevant. Otherwise the

[2] For a discussion of the difference between hard and soft determinists, see Paul Edwards, "Hard and Soft Determinism," in Sidney Hook, ed., *Determinism and Freedom* (New York, 1961), pp. 117–25, who takes these terms from William James, "The Dilemma of Determinism."

problem remains unsolved. For suppose determinism really is *incompatible* with the freedom of the will in the specified sense, say, "contra-causal freedom."[3] Then it still has to be shown that the justifiability of blame and punishment *requires* the freedom of the will in just that sense. Or suppose that determinism really is *compatible* with the freedom of the will in the specified sense, say, "absence of compulsion."[4] Then it still has to be shown that the justifiability of blame and punishment requires freedom of the will in *only* that sense. Protagonists of the opposing views continue to give proofs that determinism is or is not compatible with the freedom of the will in *their* chosen sense, but they offer no good reasons why their opponents' chosen sense should be disregarded. My main aim in this paper is to offer such reasons.

The Argument from Determinism comprises the following four steps:

(i) The advance of the sciences, showing more and more phenomena to fall under causal laws, strongly supports the claim that everything including the will is determined.

(ii) Therefore the will is not free.

(iii) Therefore no one is responsible for anything that happens.

(iv) Therefore no one ought to be punished.

Working back from the contentious conclusion, we note that the move from (iii) to (iv) requires an additional premise:

(PR) No one ought to be punished for anything unless he is responsible for it.

If (PR) is false, then (iv) does not follow from (iii) and the Argument does not have the important consequences claimed

[3] Cf. C. A. Campbell, "Is 'Freewill' a Pseudo-Problem?" *Mind*, LX (1951).

[4] Cf. Moritz Schlick, *Problems of Ethics* (New York, 1949), Ch. 7.

for it, even if (iii) follows from (i). But (PR) is false if punishment is justified in any case, whether or not the individual to whom it is meted out is responsible for that for which he is punished; or it is without much interest if punishment is unjustified in any case, whether or not the individual is responsible. If punishment is justified in any case, then the Argument from Determinism cannot succeed, for then the consequences of determinism do not touch the practice of punishment. If punishment is unjustified in any case, then the Argument from Determinism can at best succeed in driving another nail in the coffin of the practice of punishment. In order to determine the truth or falsity of (PR), we must briefly investigate what, if anything, justifies the practice of punishment and what role the responsibility of the individual punished plays in this justification.

1. *Punishment.* Punishment is a subclass of those practices which impose unwanted treatment on someone. Since from their very nature they involve doing something which is *prima facie* wrong, they require justification. Ordinarily it is sufficient justification for parents, teachers, judges who are called upon to mete out such unwanted treatment to show that they are engaged in meting out punishment. "Punishment" purports to name a justified practice. Of course, there is unjust and so unjustified punishment. But this normally means only that in an individual case something has gone wrong in the implementation: an innocent person has been found guilty, an extenuating circumstance has been overlooked, and so on. In other words, individual acts of inflicting unwanted treatment on someone would normally be shown to be justified by showing that the act was an act of punishment, i.e., that those meting out the unwanted treatment intend or at least pretend to follow all the principles governing the practice, and that none of these principles have been misapplied. The hanging of an innocent man is not an act of punishment at all if the jurymen boast they will get their man, guilty or innocent, and if the judge in full knowledge of this imposes the death sentence. But the hanging of an innocent

man is an act of punishment even if the jury merely pretend to think the man guilty. Of course, it is an unjustified act of punishment since one of the principles of punishment has been misapplied.

Thus, to show that an act is an act of punishment in which all the principles of punishment have been properly applied would normally be regarded as a justification of such an act. Inflicting unwanted treatment in accordance with the principles of punishment justifies such *prima-facie* wrong behavior. What are the principles which define the nature of the practice of punishment?

1.1 *The peculiarities of punishment.* An examination of the role of punishment in our lives shows it to be associated with two other practices, that of formulating directives to regulate the lives of individuals and that of ascertaining whether individuals have followed these directives. How essentially punishment is associated with these other practices can be seen from the fact that punishment is necessarily *for* something which must always be explained as the non-compliance with some directive. Thus, although punishing is the activity of a dispenser of unwanted treatment, it is the activity of such a dispenser within a complex system whose purpose and point hinges on the purpose and point of the directives *for* non-compliance with which the treatment is dispensed.

In the light of these few remarks we can characterize punishment as the imposition of unwanted treatment on a rational agent *for* the violation of some obligatory requirement. In every one of these respects, punishment differs importantly from other impositions of unwarranted treatment.

That it is *for* the violation of an obligatory requirement, means merely that this is the ostensible purpose or aim of the practice. It does not mean that every act of punishment in fact serves that purpose, or even that in every case the person meting out punishment must intend it to serve that purpose.

In being for the violation of an obligatory requirement, punishment differs from quarantine, military service, and taxation. By a "requirement" I mean here a subclass of rational directives expressible in terms of an ought-sentence. What subclass? Not the subclass of all those which are conclusively establishable, for it may be conclusively establishable that Jones who has a certain respiratory ailment ought to give up smoking, yet this need not be an obligation. "A requirement is obligatory" implies that it rests on grounds which make it legitimate for society to see to it that its members satisfy this requirement. When we say that it would be *wrong* for Jones not to do a certain thing, or that it is one of his *duties, obligations,* or *responsibilities* to do it, we imply that there is an obligatory requirement for him to do it.[5]

In being restricted to rational agents, punishment differs from psychiatric treatment, quarantine, and other forms of compulsory medical treatment. By "a rational agent" I here mean an agent capable of accomplishing, under a wide range of conditions, what he chooses, decides, or thinks fit to attempt, and also capable of knowing what requirements he is under and understanding the difference between legitimate and illegitimate, obligatory and non-obligatory requirements.

Thus, when we raise the question of the justifiability of punishment, we are asking not simply whether the imposition of unwanted treatment can be justified, but whether the complex practice of which punishment is a part can be justified, whether imposing unwanted treatment for violating certain sorts of social directives can be justified. Our question about punishment is linked with the larger questions of whether custom, law, morality can be justified. If such social directives cannot be justified, then practices tending to get them complied with cannot be justified, particularly if the methods are objectionable in themselves. For the purpose of this essay, I must take it for granted that there are affirmative answers to these larger questions. I shall discuss merely the question whether, given that the larger practice is justified, the practice of punishment can be justified.

[5] A full discussion of this cannot be attempted here.

Even if punishment is unjustifiable, other purposes may justify the imposition of unwanted treatment (e.g., quarantine, inoculation, taxation, military service). Thus, even if the Argument from Determinism were successful in showing the unjustifiability of punishment, it would not follow that we ought to give up the practice of imposing unwanted treatment on those who fail to conform to social regulations. For such treatment may be justifiably incorporated in practices governed by different principles.[6]

1.2 *The justification of punishment.* The two main theories in the field, utilitarian and retributive, agree that punishment is justified but differ on what justifies it and how. Utilitarian theories are frankly teleological, retributive theories tend to be anti-teleological, at least on the surface.

Utilitarian theories attempt to justify the peculiar features of the practice of punishment as well as the practice as a whole, by reference to one overall end: the holding down as far as possible of the incidence of rule-breaking. Social rules tend, from their very nature, to be broken. The *raison d'être* of punishment is to keep this tendency in check. The practice is justified to the extent to which it serves this end. Utilitarians can admit the point, usually made by retributivists, that punishment is essentially *for* the violation of an obligatory requirement, since they can construe this as a conceptual point about the nature of punishment as opposed to other forms of imposing unwanted treatment. But they must then justify that feature in terms of its effectiveness as a means to the over-all end. One such argument would be that in the absence of such a limitation governing the imposition of unwanted treatment, there would be no assurance that complying with the regulations were a protection against such treatment, hence the threat of such treatment would tend to be a less effective deterrent.[7]

[6] A few matters relevant to this point will be discussed below, section 6, pp. 81 ff.

[7] Cf. John B. Rawls on "telishment," "Two Concepts of Rules," *The Philosophical Review*, LXIV (1955).

Utilitarian justifications are capable of support or refutation by empirical evidence. Evidence showing that certain forms of punishment (e.g., capital punishment) do not deter, and that others (e.g., imprisonment) do not reform, is an argument in favor of modifications of the forms of punishment. It is conceivable that evidence may be produced to show that no form of punishment would serve the intermediate ends of deterrence and reform, and so the over-all end of keeping down the incidence of rule-breaking. In that case, punishment would have been shown to be unjustified.

The success or failure of utilitarian justifications has, however, no direct bearing on the Argument from Determinism. For if such justifications succeed, they do so only on the assumption that at least some people are responsible in the required sense. Hence if the Argument from Determinism is successful, and no one is responsible in that sense, the punishment would still be unjustified. Conversely, if such justifications fail, it is not obvious that there could not be others which might succeed.

Retributivist theories maintain that individual acts of punishment are justified if they are adequate retributions for wrong done, and the practice of punishment is justified if it is designed to mete out adequate retribution to those who have done wrong. The key to these theories thus is the correct interpretation of "retribution." Interpreted narrowly, retributivist punishment may simply be the imposition of unwanted treatment on a person who has committed a wrong and because he has committed a wrong. A utilitarian could accept this if he is then permitted to ask for a utilitarian justification of a practice so defined. It is characteristic of retributivist theories that they do not permit such a move. They tend at this stage to claim that they can just see by intuition that the world is a better place the higher the proportion of offenders who are properly punished, and a worse place the lower that proportion. Some would insist that this *is* the only consideration relevant, so that empirical evidence about the effects of punishment is entirely beside the point. Such people would not be impressed by evidence to the effect that imprisonment under our present system tends to breed hardened criminals rather than reform them. In their heaven there is more joy of the kind Lazarus felt in beholding the rich man suffering retribution in hell than there is over a sinner reformed. Other retributivists, however, might regard such evidence as relevant, if not decisive.

It is important to see that such intuitionist theories closely parallel a teleological theory which as a rule is not psychologically attractive to those who favor utilitarianism. For suppose that obligatory requirements have been properly formulated in a given society (a big *if*, of course, and too readily assumed by the pillars of most societies), then they will allot to each individual the tasks he must accomplish and the sacrifices he must make if undesirable occurrences are to be reduced, and desirable ones multiplied as much as possible. But then those who regularly satisfy such legitimate social requirements would understandably and justifiably be angry with those who do not. For by failing to do so, the rule-breakers would gain an intolerable double advantage over the rule-observers: the benefit they derive from other people's compliance and the benefit they derive from attaining their own forbidden ends. And so the righteous are perfectly justified (they have kept their part of the social bargain!) in resenting the behavior of the rule-breakers and in wishing to *vent* their resentment on them, or to have it vented vicariously and more reliably through the punitive measures of their social representatives, the judges and executioners. Now, this way of justifying punishment without reference to deterrence and reform, may not be the most elevating or edifying, but it makes a perfectly legitimate point: those who satisfy the social requirements make sacrifices which they have every moral right to expect others also to make, and those who do not satisfy them have little cause to complain if the state inflicts on them vicariously the resentment of those who have been played for suckers. On that theory, punishment is a deserved *reward* for the righteous, a deserved mollification of their resentment or demand for vengeance. Since resentment is apparently a natural phenomenon in these circumstances and since we must choose between requiring that it be suppressed by those who feel it or endured by those who cause it, a good case can be made for the latter. The case can be strengthened by a good teleological argument to the effect that, if the righteous were asked to satisfy the requirements and to suppress their resentment against those who reap dual benefits for themselves by ignoring the requirements, they would themselves be tempted to ignore them, and this would tend to disrupt the social order. On this view, punishment of wrongdoers is justified, not as a deterrent to potential violators, but as a pacifier to the righteous and so an inducement to continued compliance.

Thus, there is some empirical evidence to show that some forms of punishment currently employed do not serve some of the purposes they should serve and therefore should be reformed. However, there is no good evidence to show that no such reform is possible, and there is some evidence to suggest that the practice of punishment serves an intermediate end, the pacification of persons of (limited) good will.

2. *Responsibility.* If the practice of punishment is justified, what role does responsibility play in this justification? More specifically, is a person's being responsible for something a condition (necessary or sufficient or both) of his justifiably being punished for it?

The concept of responsibility is most easily explained in connection with our practice of holding people to account. The practices, such as punishment, which involve the infliction of essentially unwanted treatment on individuals, are particularly obnoxious if mishandled or misused. Special safeguards are therefore particularly important. Holding a person to account is designed to provide such a safeguard. As we have seen, the practice of punishment is linked with the practice of specifying, formulating, publicizing, and promulgating, as social requirements or directives or rules, those social demands which a society can expect any one of its members to satisfy, as the minimum price he must pay for the benefits accruing to him from membership in the group. The main point of the practice of holding people to account is to safeguard them, when they are accused of having failed to satisfy one of those minimal demands, against having to bear, when they do not deserve to bear it, the burden which is imposed on members who have failed to satisfy such a requirement. The practice thus interposes a number of defenses or excuses between the allegation that someone has violated an obligatory social requirement and society's imposition of the appropriate social burden on the alleged violator. Such defenses are in the nature of excusing explanations of the conduct of the accused. Many of these defenses are expressed in the words "not responsible for . . ." It will be helpful to distinguish two main senses of "responsible for," a total and a partial one. The total sense is that in which a person's being responsible for something is a *sufficient* condition of his *being subject* to, that is, rightly made to endure, a certain sort of burden or unwanted treatment; and his not being responsible a *sufficient* condition of his *not being so subject*. Remarks such as "He must bear full responsibility for the damage," "He is alone responsible for the accident," "I accept complete responsibility for the consequences" employ responsibility in that total sense. To indicate that a person has responsibility for something in that total sense, I shall say that he is *liable for it*, and I shall indicate the nature of the burden *to* which this liability makes him subject by the word "to," as in "liable to punishment." Thus, the claim that Jones is liable for damages usually means that because of the damage he has done he is liable at least to "compulsory indemnification" and if criminally liable, also to punishment.

The partial sense of "responsible for"[8] is that in which a person's not being responsible is a *sufficient* condition of his not being subject to this sort of burden, and his being responsible a *necessary* but not also a sufficient condition of

[8] This explanation does not include "causally responsible for" which is discussed below, p. 64.

59

his being so subject. We can distinguish three different types of case: accountability, answerability, and culpability. A man is *accountable* if he is a rational agent in the sense of being able to have ends which, on the basis of deliberation he finds best to have, and of being able to pursue and attain these. A man is *answerable* for a particular happening if it is due to his failure to satisfy an obligatory requirement. A man is *culpable* if the explanation of his failure to satisfy a requirement is inculpatory rather than exculpatory. These forms specify, respectively, the type of agents capable of being liable, the range of failures for which such agents become liable, and the range of explanations of such failures which do *not* exculpate and so make liable those agents who have failed.

An example may help. Jones accuses Smith of having driven above the speed limit and ignored a traffic light, thus causing a collision with and bodily injury to Jones as well as damage to Jones' car. Morally speaking, anyone can be accused of anything, though of course he should not be accused without adequate evidence. A person accused should defend himself, if he can. Legally speaking, accusation is a public enterprise and so "arraignability" depends on the satisfaction of certain conditions which, however, are satisfied in almost all cases. Typical exceptions are being an infant, or having diplomatic status. Once arraigned, Smith, through his advocate, can establish non-responsibility and so exoneration, by showing that he was *non-accountable*, e.g., a minor or a madman. If Smith fails in this he can attempt to prove that it was not he who collided with Jones, and so he was not answerable and so *not responsible* for it. If he fails in this, Smith can attempt to show that, though he did these things, he was not required not to do them (as when Smith claims he was driving an ambulance). Even if he fails in all these defenses and has to admit that he failed to do what he was required to do, he can still attempt to prove that he was not responsible, since *not culpable,* by providing an exonerating or at least extenuating explanation of why he acted in the way he did; for instance, if he is a plain-clothes policeman pursuing criminals or if he is one of our spies coming in from the cold pursued by enemy police. If, finally, all possible defenses are exhausted, the accused must be found guilty and so held responsible for the mishap, and hence liable to punishment.

2.1. For our purposes, the best way to explain the connection between these cases is to begin with culpability. When we say that Smith was not responsible for the accident because his brakes failed, we usually mean that, although the accident would not have happened if he had not acted as he did (but had swung the car round instead of stepping on the brakes, let us say), he is not culpable and so at any rate not liable to punishment, even though he may be liable to "compulsory indemnification," that is, obligated to pay for the damage caused by the accident. When a person is blamed for something, he can attempt to avert liability by offering a certain type of explanation of his behavior (e.g., "I did not know that my brakes were not working") and so prove that he is not culpable, or if so, culpable to a low degree. Thus while his behavior will of course always have an explanation, not every type of explanation exculpates. Sometimes, on the contrary, an explanation inculpates the agent if it shows that his will was aimed at something, the attainment of which is held to be or to involve the infringement of some requirement; and he is the more culpable the more "directly" his will[9] is aimed at such an infringement. If the agent actually *intends* to violate the requirement, the highest degree of culpability is incurred, particularly if it is a prohibition against inflicting harm, e.g., killing, assaulting, stealing, and so forth. He is less culpable if he does not want to do these things but knows that what he wants to attain unavoidably involves a violation of some requirement; even less so if he merely wantonly or recklessly risks its violation; less so still if he merely fails to take the necessary precautions to eliminate

[9] The will is a wider notion than intention. The will is most directly involved if one does something deliberately or carries out an intention or plan. It is involved less "directly" if one neglects to do something one ought to do.

such risks. The less "directly" the agent aims at the violation of the requirement, the lower the degree of his culpability, and hence the smaller the burden to which he becomes liable. Clearly, this connection between responsibility, culpability, and liability to punishment is justifiable on either the retributive or the teleological theory of punishment. The principle involved seems to be this: that we punish people to the extent that their *wills* (not their movements) are causally responsible for the violation of a requirement.[10]

The explanation of an agent's failure to do what is claimed to be required of him is exculpatory if it shows that it is due not to the badness of the agent's will; that is, its being directed at the violation of a requirement, but that it has occurred in spite of the goodness of the agent's will. There are two importantly different types of such exculpatory explanation. There are those which show that the agent wanted to satisfy the requirement and failed because of insuperable obstacles, for example, lack of strength, equipment, skill, knowledge (as when Smith failed to catch the thief because he was not fast enough). And there are those which show that the agent did indeed aim at the violation of the requirement but only because aiming at its satisfaction would have involved intrinsically unwanted consequences for himself (as when he fails to run after the thief because the man beside him is holding a gun at his head). Both inculpatory explanations and this second type of exculpatory one therefore have this in common: in both cases it is the agent's intention not to satisfy a requirement. But there is this difference between them. In the case of inculpatory ones, the reason why the agent fails to satisfy a requirement is that he thereby hopes to attain a benefit for himself. In the case of these exculpatory ones, the reason why he fails is that he hopes thereby to avoid something intrinsically unwanted for him-

---

[10] For an explanation of "causally responsible for," see below, p. 64. For a discussion of the acceptability of such a principle to a utilitarian, see P. H. Nowell-Smith, "Freewill and Moral Responsibility," *Mind,* LVII (1948).

self. Typical cases are torture and the threat of it, or psychological and physiological exertion, as when a man has to resist an inclination or urge, or has to perform a laborious task to satisfy the requirement.[11]

Clearly, this connection too between responsibility, culpability, and liability is justifiable on either theory of punishment, since the underlying principle of exculpation (the principle that the agent ought not to be punished if he has adequate reasons for ignoring the requirement) is accepted by both theories. We do not regard a person as justified in securing for himself a gain if he has to inflict hardship on another. For the same reason we consider a requirement the less justifiable and so the less obligatory the more its satisfaction imposes hardship on those who satisfy it.

2.2. In the light of these remarks, it is easy to see the connection between answerability and culpability. Clearly, the question of culpability or guiltlessness cannot arise independently of at least the allegation of an agent's failure to satisfy a requirement, and there is normally no call to raise the question of culpability until there is proof or at least good evidence that some agent has failed to satisfy an obligatory requirement. Thus we cannot say that because he was involved in an accident, Smith is to blame for it and so liable to punishment because culpable, until we have shown that the accident is something for which Smith is *answerable*, that is, something for which he *must* give an exculpatory explanation in order to escape liability to punishment. And we cannot show that he is answerable for the accident until we have shown that the accident is something or is the consequence of something which Smith was required to prevent (as an operator of a night club may be required to prevent the outbreak of a fire),[12] or to refrain from bringing about (as a motorist is required to refrain from charging into

[11] For further details, see below, pp. 71 ff.

[12] Cf. the case of *Commonwealth v. Welansky*, as reprinted in *Freedom and Responsibility; Readings in Philosophy and Law*, Herbert Morris, ed. (Stanford, 1961), pp. 233–38.

another car because he is required to refrain from bringing about damage to another car), or from doing (as a motorist is required to refrain from driving through a traffic light). When an accusation is made against someone, three points must first be established: (a) that there really exists an obligatory requirement of a certain sort, moral, legal, customary; (b) that it is a requirement applying to the accused; (c) that the accused has engaged in behavior which constitutes a violation of this requirement. When they are established, it is proved that the accused person is answerable for something, that he must produce an exculpatory explanation or else be liable.

2.21. Here someone may object that I have left out an important element, namely, the causal connection between what the agent is doing and the events he brings about and so is said to be responsible for (in yet another sense of "responsible"). Jones, who is pressing the bell, this objector may say, "is (causally) responsible for" the ringing. But this objection can be ignored because this narrow causal sense of "responsible for" is not central to our problem. Rational agents can think ahead and so their responsibility extends beyond what they are doing, beyond the events they are bringing about or preventing, to things they could have done, brought about or prevented if this were required of them. It is only when they are required to *refrain* from doing something (e.g., arson) that failure to satisfy the requirement will mean that they are causally responsible as well as answerable for what happens. In many cases the requirement is that we take positive action of some sort (e.g., the night watchman's duty to sound the fire alarm) and in cases of this sort those who do not satisfy the requirement are answerable for precisely what they *failed* to cause to happen.

This point is obscured by the great variety of ways in which obligatory requirements are formulated. We can classify these formulations on the basis of two determinables: (a) the generality or specificity of the manner in which the person *who* has the requirement is specified, and (b) the extent of forethought and circumspection needed for satisfying the requirement.

(a) When we say that killing, stealing, lying, adultery, and not helping another in need are *wrong*, we indicate in a perfectly general way the agents to whom these requirements apply. We do so by indicating the kind of thing *any* and *every* agent *must* refrain from doing or *must* do. By contrast, when we specify duties, obligations, or responsibilities, we typically indicate what a particular person, or class of persons, must do or must refrain from doing. They must do these things or refrain from doing them, not because any other kind of behavior would in itself be wrong, but because, although it would not be wrong, it is the duty, obligation, or responsibility of these particular agents, and not of others, to do these things, and therefore (and only for this reason) not doing them would be wrong.

(b) When we say that killing or that neglecting one's duties is wrong, we indicate requirements which can be satisfied with comparatively little forethought and circumspection, simply by *doing* or by refraining from doing a certain thing. By contrast, when we say that irresponsibility or inconsiderateness or recklessness is wrong, we refer to requirements whose satisfaction involves forethought and circumspection, which cannot be satisfied simply by doing something but only by bringing some things about and by preventing others, by seeing to it that certain things are done by certain people or provided or seen to by them, not by merely obeying orders and discharging routine tasks, but by thinking ahead, giving orders, organizing things.[13]

These two ways of specifying requirements must be kept apart. The degree of forethought, circumspection and care required of one person to avoid doing wrong by doing something which causes harm to another is considerably lower than that which some other person may have to employ for the same purpose, if he has special duties, obligations, or

[13] Cf. the interesting paper by J. Roland Pennock, "The Problems of Responsibility," *Nomos*, III (1960).

responsibilities. In all these cases, cases in which agents have failed to exercise the circumspection, care, and forethought required of them in connection with complex or negative tasks, a person may fail to satisfy a requirement, be answerable for a variety of disasters, be culpable and liable, yet not be in any way "causally responsible" for them.[14]

2.3. Lastly, a guardian can claim on behalf of his ward, or an advocate on behalf of his client, that he is not accountable, that is, that he lacks those properties in virtue of which alone a person can justifiably be held to account for anything including his own actions. If anyone lacks these properties, then he cannot become liable to punishment, since he cannot understand what a requirement is, let alone the difference between legitimate and illegitimate ones, cannot know what the various requirements are, which of them apply to him and when, and how he would go about satisfying or violating them, and is therefore not able to take such information into account in his deliberations about what to do, if indeed he is capable of any such deliberations. It is not difficult to see why non-responsibility, in the sense of non-accountability, should be regarded as a sufficient condition of non-liability to punishment. On both theories of punishment, individual cases of punishment are inflictions of intrinsically unwanted treatment on those and only those who have behaved in ways which they understand to be violations of obligatory requirements applying to them. Considering the content of obligatory requirements and the temptation which rational agents must frequently feel to ignore them in order to attain greater benefits for themselves, it is perfectly clear why both theories of punishment can and should subscribe to a definition which limits the practice to accountable agents.

2.4. To sum up, "Punishment," as we have seen, carries the implication that the practice of which it is the name is the justified, socially organized infliction, under narrowly circumscribed conditions, of intrinsically unwanted treatment,

[14] Cf. again *Commonwealth v. Welensky, loc. cit.*

and that it is the observation of these limiting conditions which confers on individual cases of punishment the *justification* for the practice. Like some other justified practices of inflicting unwanted treatment on people, the practice of punishment is tied to the practice of holding people to account. This ensures that accusations do not lead to the infliction of such unwanted treatment unless all three of the conditions of liability (the justifiability of its infliction) are met, namely, accountability, answerability, and culpability. The fact that a person can show that he is *not responsible* in any one of *these three senses* for that of which he has been accused is sufficient to show that he is not liable to punishment for this, and so ought not to be punished for it, so that it is unnecessary to investigate the other two conditions.

3. In the light of this discussion, we can now see that (PR) is true in any one of the four senses of "responsible for" which we distinguished, namely, accountable, answerable, culpable, and liable. It is, however, not true if it is interpreted to mean "causally responsible for." I take it for granted, without argument, that (PR) is not true in yet another, the forward-looking, requirement-stating sense of "responsible for," as in "Jones is responsible for supplies." This type of remark gives information about *what* a certain man is required to do, or who is required to do a certain thing, without as yet raising any accusation, claiming any violation, or blaming anyone for anything. And there are no doubt other senses of "responsible for" in which (PR) is false. But the four senses indicated seem to me the only senses related to the practice of holding people to account before imposing any burden on them, and so to that subclass of it which is punishment.

It needs to be made clear that we are discussing the justification, not of *all* infliction of unwelcome treatment but of punishment—that is of treatment *designed* to be unwelcome. Responsibility is, at most, a necessary condition of the justifiability of treatment whose very purpose is to be unwelcome. It cannot be thought a necessary condition of the justifiability of quarantine or military service although these may in fact be just as unwelcome to those concerned as penal sanctions would be. Thus even if no one is responsible for anything there may still be other justifications for inflicting on individuals treatment which, until we can find ways to make the army or the quarantine hospital more attractive, they may in fact dislike.

We can now return to our main problem: Can we infer (iv), that no one ought to be punished, from the fact (PR), that no one ought to be punished for anything unless he is responsible for it, and the fact (iii), that no one is responsible for anything? That clearly depends on whether the senses of "responsible," if any, in which (iii) is true, include the senses in which (PR) is true. And this depends on just what kind of "bondage of the will" is implied by determinism.

Most philosophers have interpreted the bondage of the will to be a condition or state of all agents which implies their guiltlessness. They have in other words taken (iii) to mean that the unfreedom of the will, which is supposed to follow from determinism, constitutes *a universal exonerating explanation* of all human behavior. They have taken (iii) to amount to this: When in an individual case the will of a person is not free, on a particular occasion, then on that occasion he is not to blame for what he did, he is not responsible, and so not liable to punishment; therefore if quite generally the will is not free, then everyone is always in that blameless position, and so nobody is ever liable to punishment. An examination of (iii) will involve, in the first place, an examination of the various types of exonerating explanation, and in the second place, an examination of whether determinism implies that such exonerating explanations are available for everything anyone ever does.

4. First I shall consider explanations showing that a person is not responsible because not *culpable*. As has already been said, such exculpatory explanations naturally fall into two categories: those which claim that the agent was *not able*, and those which claim that, in a certain sense, he was *not free* to do anything else. That the will is not free has been inter-

preted to constitute a universal exculpatory explanation belonging to *either* of these categories.

4.1. I begin with explanations of the *first category*, the agent's *inability* to act otherwise than he did.[15] Ordinarily, this kind of explanation is confined to a limited class of cases, characterizable in certain specific ways, of which the following three are the most obvious types, and which have served as the main models of the kind of bondage we all would supposedly suffer if determinism were true: irresistible force (section 4.11), superior strategy (section 4.12), unavoidability (section 4.13).

4.11. Some people are prevented from going to work by being dragged in handcuffs to a police station, from straightening their leg by a cramp. In such cases, the agent does not have sufficient muscular strength or skill to overcome the forces to which he is being subjected, and so fails to do anything toward his goals. In the end, what happens is an involuntary movement, not something done by him.

4.12. At the beginning of a chess game, the Grandmaster may, for the fun of it, predict that he will checkmate his opponent on the thirty-fourth move at a particular square. The novice is nowhere succumbing to irresistible force, not only are his movements completely voluntary, but what he does is done intentionally, perhaps with a plan in mind. Nevertheless, in the end he is trapped, defeated, and forced to do things he does not *want* to do. On some fatalistic theories, the explanation of some events is that they are fated or predestined to come about, that is, they occur because some invisible and powerful intelligence is "guiding" the events in the world, in much the way a chessmaster or superior general is conducting a campaign. It is quite a sensible corollary of this view of the world that it does not much matter what an individual does or does not do, for the important events are destined to happen anyway, and he cannot know which events are so predestined.

---

[15] Cf. G. E. Moore, *Ethics* (Oxford, 1949), Ch. VII.

4.13. Sometimes, *the circumstances* impose limits of maneuverability so narrow that there is no way for an agent to achieve his end. In such a case, he can say, in relation to what happens—which is other than what he wants to happen—that he could not help it, that it was unavoidable. A motorist running over a child in the street, a man trapped in a boat drifting in the current and landing on a private beach, may not be able to help any of these things: they may have been unavoidable, in the circumstances.

On this interpretation of "the will is not free," every failure of an agent to satisfy a requirement has the same exculpatory explanation as in cases in which there is some difficulty or obstacle which, with the best will in the world, he cannot surmount. However, if this is the correct interpretation of "free will," then the Argument from Determinism fails. It could succeed only if determinism entailed that, in all cases when human beings fail to satisfy an obligatory social requirement, the explanation is that it was their end to satisfy it but they were unable to do so. But determinism is no less compatible with cases in which someone fails to satisfy a requirement simply *because it is not his end* to do so than it is with cases in which he fails to satisfy it, *although it is his end* to do so. Hence determinism cannot entail that all explanations are of the latter rather than of the former kind. Thus on this interpretation of "the will is not free," although (ii) implies (iii), (ii) cannot support (iii) since (ii) does not follow from (i).

So far we have seen that determinism does not entail that the excuse "he wanted to do the right thing but was unable to" is available to everyone who fails to satisfy a requirement. A determinist might try to argue, however, that, although all "offenders" do not have this excuse, they have one something like it, namely, that whether or not their intentions were good, *they could not have acted differently.* This is a legitimate extension of section 4.13. For if no one ever could have acted differently from the way he did, if no one ever could have helped doing what he did, then the distinction we ordinarily draw between those whose intentions are good and those whose intentions are bad loses its point. For that distinction is drawn on the assumption that having a different intention from the one a person has would often make a difference to what he does.

What is the sense of "he could have acted differently," which is involved in this assumption? It is a trivial one. In it, from the fact that an agent *did* something, it *follows* that he could have done something else. Suppose it granted that Jones' handing over $100 to charity was something he did, then it follows that there must be some other causally possible chain of events (i.e., compatible with causal laws, not compatible with both the laws and *all* the events), say, Jones' handing over $50 to charity which, if it had happened instead, would be something Jones did. The crucial point is that these alternative, causally possible chains of events must be capable of action-explanations relating to Jones as the agent. An agent, in this context, is a creature tending to have goal-directed propensities, that is, propensities to respond to a range of stimuli in a goal-directed manner. Action-descriptions (e.g., "he raised his arm" rather than "his arm went up") are applied to such responses. Of such responses it must be possible to give action-explanations, that is, explanations in which what the agent aims at, and his relevant beliefs, are determining factors. It is a defining characteristic of agents of the sort we have in mind (animals, children, servomechanisms, normal adults) that, for a large range of conditions and goals, the necessary conditions of success, that is, of the goal-directed responses leading to the attainment of the goal, are satisfied. For the normal range of such goals and of conditions under which they are pursued and reached, we can refer to these conditions quite independently of whether at a given time the agent has the goal for whose attainment their satisfaction is necessary. We can, moreover, classify them under various heads, such as talents, know-how, physical strength, information, opportunity, absence of obstacles, resoluteness. When we say that an agent *can* do something, we imply that some or all of the necessary conditions of success are satisfied, without necessarily implying that the agent actually has the goal.

Thus, if someone did something, he necessarily could have done something else instead. For he would not be an agent, in the required sense, if at any time there were nothing at all he could do instead of what he is actually "doing." Hence even that which he is actually "doing" should not be described as something he *did*.[16]

Does it follow from determinism that no one in this sense does anything, or is agency in this sense compatible with determinism? I cannot attempt a complete answer to that question. I do not think such an answer is necessary. It is sufficient to say that, as I have characterized agency, there can be no more incompatibility between it and determinism than there is between thermostatically-controlled heating systems, or self-aiming anti-aircraft guns, or other state-maintaining servomechanisms and determinism. Of course, built-in randomizers and the like give rise to interesting problems, but these are outside the range that has exercised the moralists.

Here an important objection may be raised. From the fact that a person did something, it cannot follow (contrary to what I say) that he could have done something else, since he may not have been able to *help doing what he did* (as when a motorist runs over a child).[17] But this is to misunderstand the point, for that he could have acted differently does not mean that it is true for *any* action-description of what he did, that he could have acted differently: this need be true only for *some* action-descriptions, for example, he could have turned the wheel the other way, or he could have stepped on the accelerator rather than the brakes. It may be thought that this would not be enough to meet the requirements of liability. For a person who acts in a way which fails to satisfy a requirement must be able to act not merely differently but

[16] There is not space here to go into detail. I have said more on this topic in "Could and Would," *Analysis*, XXIII, Supp. No. 1 (1963), and in "Action and Agent," *Monist*, XLIX (April 1965).

[17] See above, section 4.13.

in a way which satisfies the requirement. The fact that he could have stepped on the accelerator must leave untouched the fact that this would not have prevented his running over the child. This is of course true, but beside the point. For if he can show that he could not meet the requirement, that is, could not avoid running over the child, then this constitutes an *exculpatory* explanation. However, such an explanation will apply only in virtue of the particular circumstances. It cannot be derived for all cases from the truth of determinism.

But, it may now be asked, what is the importance of this sense of "agency"? The proof that men are agents in this sense does not show that their will is free in any interesting sense. This is true. However, my account of agency yields a categorical sense of "can" in terms of which it is true that such agents categorically can do things which they are not actually doing, and all this in perfect harmony with determinism. Moreover, there is only one other step needed to take us from this comparatively uninteresting type of agency to the more interesting ones exemplified by human beings. In our account of agency, we did not indicate how an agent comes to have those goal-directed propensities which are the mark of agency. Some agents are what might be called "slaves of the passions," that is, agents whose goal-directed propensities are determined in accordance with the balance of the strongest psychological forces[18] pressing on them. In their case, there is no scope for the will or practical reason. Others are rational agents, in whom such goal-directed propensities are determined through deliberation and choice. The former could have acted differently *if and only if* they had wanted to. The latter could have acted differently *if* they had *but* wanted to *and even if* they had not wanted to. They also could have acted differently if they had *but chosen*. In a rational agent, such if-clauses indicate not the necessary, nor the necessary and sufficient, but a sufficient condition (given the satisfac-

[18] For an explanation of this term, see below, section 4.2, pp. 74 f.

tion of the other normally satisfied conditions) of the agent's coming to have a goal-directed propension.

4.2. *Second category* of exculpatory explanations. The most natural, though by no means the most widely employed interpretation of "the will is not free," refers to cases in which a person could (if he wanted) have satisfied the requirements laid upon him, but where he did not want to because his will was under exculpatory pressure. In these cases, such failure really is due to the malorientation of his will. Yet, because the malorientation is not due to his having a bad will, the explanation constitutes an excuse. Before I turn to the various specific excuses under this head, we must distinguish three types of pressure on an individual, all involving what might be called psychological force: (a) Irresistible urge, (b) Irresistible desire, and (c) Prospect of being subjected to psychological force.

(a) When I put my hand in the fire or hold my breath, the discomfort increases until it becomes unbearable and I let go. This must be distinguished from the cases where there is a mere reflex response. It might have been arranged in such a way (as with the patellar reflex) that when there is a stimulus of a certain kind and magnitude, the reflex goes into operation, without there being any urge. No urge is literally irresistible. Scaevola allowed his hand to burn up, some people are said to have held their breath until they fainted. But society allows a certain intensity of discomfort or pain to constitute a valid excuse for letting go.

(b) Irresistible desires differ from irresistible urges chiefly in this, that they involve consciously goal-directed action, and not merely a letting go. A person need not learn to yield to an urge but must learn to resist it. By contrast, a person must first learn how to satisfy cravings and desires before he can learn to resist them. Thus, whereas a person's intelligence is necessarily involved only in resisting urges, not in yielding to them, it is necessarily involved in satisfying desires as well as in resisting them. Morons have no problems about satisfying their urges, but they have great problems about satisfying even simple desires.

Whereas the question of the resistibility or irresistibility of an urge can arise in all cases when a person has an urge, this is not so in the case of a desire, for where a desire cannot be satisfied, as when a hungry person has nothing to eat, the question of whether to give in or to resist does not arise. Where it does arise, the answer is of the same sort as in the case of urges.

(c) The concept of a desire can be used to explain the idea of psychological force. When a person knows or has beliefs about what course of action would remove an acute current discomfort and/or bring pleasurable experiences, or both, we can speak, without I think being seriously misleading, of his being subjected to psychological force in the direction of that course of action. "The will" is primarily used to refer to the ability to satisfy requirements in the face of pressures from currently experienced or anticipated psychological forces (as in the case of threat of torture or the existence of sanctions). It is in these contexts that questions of its power and strength, weakness, and inadequacy normally arise.

We can now turn to the three main cases of excuse involving pressure on a person's will, that is, pressure to pursue or abandon a certain goal: Coercion (section 4.21), Compulsion by circumstances (section 4.22), Compulsion from within (section 4.23).

4.21. Coercion. Under this heading we include all cases in which "the will is not free" is interpreted as a double generalization, both for agents and for times, of the expression, "When A did x, he did not do it of his own free will." This refers to cases in which an agent does something under orders, duress, or even posthypnotic suggestion, though not what he does under hypnosis, certain drugs, or during sleepwalking. In such cases what A does is done intentionally, but the intention is formed under psychological pressure (e.g., torture or threat of torture) from another person, B. In such cases, failure to satisfy a requirement is a failure of the will.

What makes this explanation of the failure an excuse, never-theless, is the fact that this failure is not due to an inherent malorientation of A's will but to unjustified pressure from B. If the situation calls for punishment at all, it calls for punish-ment primarily of B, not necessarily of A. Hence this ex-planation of A's failure constitutes an excuse, and possibly an exoneration of A.

Now, in individual cases, this excuse works well enough, but it cannot be universalized, as it stands. For if determin-ism is true, any other person has the same excuse, and so the fault-shifting would have to go on *ad infinitum*. I conclude that, if "the will is not free" is the universalization of "When A did x, he did not do it of his own free will," then (iii) can-not be true since the excuse literally cannot be universalized. And so (iv) derives no support from (iii) thus interpreted.

4.22. Compulsion by circumstances. There is another equally natural interpretation of "the will is not free." That phrase may be read as the universalization of "When A did x, his will was not free," and this may be taken to cover those cases of intentionally doing x in which we say that the agent was compelled, obliged, forced, or had to do x. We could make any of these claims in the case when, having missed the last bus, and having no other means of transportation, A had to take a taxi, that is, had to take a taxi in order to get home. This does not of course mean that A could not have sat on a bench in the park or walked all night if he had wanted or decided to. All it means is that in order to get home, as he wanted to, the only acceptable means available to him was a cab.

Clearly, universalization of this excuse is unproblematic, for we are not now dealing with that special case of compulsion, or coercion, in which the compelling factor originates in a second human will. However, now the question arises whether this is necessarily an excuse, even in individual cases. For there are cases where we can accept the facts stated in a person's claim that he was, in this sense, compelled to do x, but where nevertheless we should not accept his claim as an excuse. Thus, if he has an obligation to save money, then the fact that he could not get home in any other "acceptable" way need be no excuse for taking a taxi. It all depends on the legitimacy and seriousness of the requirement when compared with the effort, troublesomeness, and harmfulness of what is involved in satisfying it. The requirement may be serious enough to warrant his asking his host to put him up, or to sit all night on a bench in the park, or even to walk all the way home. And if I am right in this, then (iii) is not sound for this interpretation of "free will." For either the lack of free will means no more than that there is only one way for the agent to attain his end, whatever it may be, or it also implies something about the relative merits of achieving that end in this way and abandoning it altogether. If it means the former, then it does not always constitute an excuse. Raskolnikov was not *compelled* to kill the old woman and so had no excuse for doing so, even though killing her was the only means of getting her money. And if it means the latter, it is most implausible to suggest that determinism implies that the will is not free in that sense. How could it follow from determinism that *every* agent *always* has only *one* way of attaining his end, *and* that it is always *better* that he should pursue and attain his end in that way rather than abandon the end?

4.23. Compulsion from within. The cases to be discussed in this section have affinities with cases of coercion in that they involve the agent's being subjected to pressure by psychological forces, or his belief that he will be unless he acts in certain prophylactic ways, but differ from them in that the pressure or threat of pressure does not come from other human wills.

Let us, for argument's sake, grant the highly implausible factual claim that every agent who fails to satisfy a requirement, fails (if determinism is true) because he is being subjected to pressure by actual or anticipated psychological forces of varying magnitudes but *sufficient* to overcome his will. Now surely this does not constitute a universal excuse. On the contrary, where the pressure of psychological forces is small, yet big enough to overcome the agent's will to satisfy the requirement in question, we speak of weakness of will and regard this as a justification for blame and as a ground for punishment. Unlike weakness of biceps, weakness of will is not an exculpatory explanation!

There is, moreover, the following important distinction to be drawn. Agents exposed to such pressures may or may not know how to avoid getting into and how to shake off the grip of these forces too strong for them to resist. If they know this, their being in their grip is itself something calling for an excuse, which they may or may not be able to provide. If they do not know how, or though knowing it, have an excuse, then they must be regarded as having an unfortunate, but non-culpable weakness or illness of the will which, like an infectious disease, is dangerous to others, and so may and should be treated appropriately, though not by punishment.

It is sometimes suggested that the fact that a person cannot want to do a certain thing or cannot help wanting not to do it constitutes an exculpatory explanation, both of not doing what he does not want to do, and of not wanting to do it, even when there is an obligatory requirement to do it. All these arguments rest on simple confusions.

Let us first distinguish between two senses of "wanting to," namely, "desiring" and "having a preponderant goal-directed propensity." Taking the sense of "desire" first, it will only very seldom if ever be the case that an agent's not actually having a certain desire will make it impossible for him to do a certain thing. Perhaps crown princes have sometimes for this reason been unable to perform their marital duties and were thereby excused. However, there is now a great deal of practical wisdom, available in paperback, on a great variety of desires, so that the conscientious person can acquire and arouse such desires by diligent methods. This makes the excuse of not having the necessary desire the less available.

The second sense is more important. If Jones does not have

a certain preponderant goal-directed propensity (intention, determination, resolve), such as being bent on winning a race, then he *will not* put up a good show. But this does not mean that he *cannot* put up a good show. For though he probably cannot *without* coming to have such a propensity, a normal agent normally can come to have it, by no greater an effort than the simple process of rational deliberation about what to do. In such a case, not having such a propensity is no excuse. It is only those few who are "slaves of their passions" or in the grip of an irresistible desire who cannot produce such propensities at will. For some of these, not having the propensity will constitute an excuse, for others it will not, as was explained above. In any case, the truth of determinism cannot show that everybody has such an excuse.

Summing up, we can say that (ii) does not support (iii), if the unfreedom of the will implies merely that the strength of individual wills must always be inadequate to overcome the pressure of those psychological forces which would have to be overcome if a requirement is to be satisfied—for weakness of will is not an excuse. Again, (ii) does not support (iii) if the unfreedom of the will shows merely that all agents who fail to satisfy a requirement have got into the grip of psychological forces so strong that no agent could reasonably be expected to overcome them, since having got into that grip does not necessarily excuse the inabilities so acquired. Again, (ii) does not support (iii) if the unfreedom of the will implies merely that some agents did not want to do what was required of them, in the sense of having no desire or intention of doing it.

However, (ii) really does support (iii) if the will's being unfree implies that all agents who fail to satisfy requirements have unavoidably fallen into the grip of such psychological forces and inescapably remain in it. Can determinism show that everyone who fails to satisfy a requirement is in this last condition? It is sometimes argued that people could have acted differently if they had wanted, but that they could not have wanted if determinism is true.[19] From this some deduce that people could never have acted differently from the way they did. The conclusion seems to follow because the crucial if-clause is misinterpreted to mean "only if they could have wanted." If this did follow, then determinism really would provide an exculpatory explanation on the grounds of inability, as under section 4.1. However, that excuse is clearly inapplicable here, for the present case is one in which a person *ex hypothesi does not want to satisfy* the requirement, hence inability is not relevant. In any case, an agent's ability to do something does not depend on his ability to want to do it. An agent's inability to *want* to pay his taxes may or may not be an exculpatory explanation of his *refusal* to pay them, but it cannot prove his *inability* to pay them. Such a person may be excusably or justifiably *unwilling* to pay them, but he is not *unable* to pay them. Moreover, if it is desirable that he should pay them and so that he should want to pay them, and if making him liable to punishment will make him willing to pay them, then the fact that (if determinism is true) his wanting to pay them was ruled out, as things were, does not militate against his being held liable for not *paying*.

Others simply derive the conclusion that, because people's wants are causally determined, no one could have wanted anything other than he did want, and so no one is to blame for the wants he has and so, by implication, for what he does, which is determined by his wants.

Now, we can grant that if determinism is true, then in a sense no one could have wanted anything other than what he did want. But the sense is the comparatively trivial one in which he "could have" means "it was consequentially possible that he should have," and "he could not have" means "it was consequentially impossible that he should have" or, in other words, "he would not have unless some matters had been

[19] Cf. discussion in G. E. Moore, *Ethics*, Ch. VI; J. L. Austin, "Ifs and Cans," *Proceedings of the British Academy*, XLII (1956), pp. 109–32; P. H. Nowell-Smith, *Ethics* (Baltimore, 1954), Chs. 19 and 20.

different earlier on." But from the fact that no one could have wanted anything other than he did want, no interesting consequence can be derived. It cannot for instance disprove that, had people wanted to, they could have used certain techniques to acquire or arouse certain desires, or engaged in deliberation and so acquired those propensities which were needed to satisfy the requirement which they did not in fact satisfy. Thus, even if determinism could show that all agents who fail to satisfy requirements do so because they are in the grip of forces too strong for them to resist, it cannot show that they are necessarily exculpated. For it fails to show that they inevitably fall into the grip of these forces. They may have got into their grip only because they failed to have those wants, summed up as "the good will," directed toward doing what is possible to satisfy the requirements. It is because they fail to have this that we hold them liable.

I conclude that determinism cannot show that the will is in bondage in a sense which would constitute an exculpatory explanation of all those cases in which accountable agents have failed to do what is obligatorily required of them.

5. No popular interpretation of "free will" relates to our second excuse, *answerability;* indeed it is difficult to see how a case could be made for saying that, if determinism is true, nobody is obligatorily required to do anything and so not answerable for anything. I therefore ignore it.

6. *Accountability.* It is now time to consider our third sense of responsibility, namely, accountability. We must answer two questions: For what sense of "freedom of the will" is that freedom a condition of or entailed by accountability? (section 6.1) Can determinism imply that the will is not free in this sense? (section 6.2)

6.1. Non-accountability is not so much a bondage of the will as a flaw in practical reason. We have seen that non-accountable agents are those who cannot understand what a requirement is, and so cannot be taught a lesson for violating such a requirement, although they may be able to profit in other ways from the infliction of undesirable treatment, and should perhaps, if they are dangerous, have it administered for the protection of others. But this would not amount to punishment.

Accountability thus is that state of rationality in which an agent can understand why there are requirements and why there are sanctions for them, and can so regulate his life that he can, if he wishes, comply with the requirements and so avoid the sanctions. Producing this central want, the good will, is one of the main tasks of education. If an agent is not accountable, he cannot acquire the good will, and therefore cannot so conduct his life, and hence is rightly not held to account, not held liable to punishment.

6.2. Can determinism show that there are no such rational agents? Two claims are involved: that nobody has the requisite understanding or that nobody is able to act in accordance with it.

The main argument goes as follows. Granted that a person can satisfy his wants and do as he pleases; granted that he can act in accordance with his decisions and his choices; even so he finds himself with his natural inclinations and desires, with his temperament and his character, which in turn determine his choices and decisions. Put in this form, the argument in effect calls in question the legitimacy and obligatoriness of requirements. If the obligatoriness of social requirements can be salvaged, then a society is justified in inculcating in their young a good will, and everything else follows from this. If this argument cannot be met, then our social system is without justification and we impose obligatory requirements without having the right to do so. But that problem does not seem to hinge on the truth of determinism.

Put in another form, the argument is simply a variant of one used before, under section 4.2. The main difference is that instead of "if he had wanted to" it uses "if he had chosen." Now, the question is whether a person who has made one choice could have made another instead, and again the claim is that if determinism is true, he could not have chosen differently.

My reply is that determinism is perfectly compatible with there being rational agents, that is, agents whose preponderant goal-directed propensities often are determined by the outcome of preceding deliberations. But if someone is such a rational agent, then from the fact that he has made a certain choice, it logically follows that he could have made another choice. For he could not have made any choice, if he had not had a choice to make, that is, had not been confronted by alternatives between which to choose. But given that he has the ability to choose and has a choice to make, it follows that he can choose any of the alternatives confronting him. Admittedly, in a particular case, the psychological make-up of the agent might put some of the alternatives open to him beyond the strength of his will. But this is a matter of individual psychology, not a consequence of determinism. Of course, from this it does not follow (what would be incompatible with determinism) that he might have actually made another choice *even if everything had been the same.* But the impossibility of that (guaranteed by determinism) can hardly be regarded as a limitation on the power or freedom of choice, or on the will. For imagine that someone, after deliberation, chose the house with the view and the large spare room. Responsibility can hardly require the possibility that *even if everything had been just as it was,* he should have chosen the one without the view and with the small spare room. Surely choice is and ought to be determined by the relevant facts. Determinism cannot show that a rational agent who has a choice cannot choose any of the alternatives from which he has a choice to make. But neither can it show that rational agents never have choices to make. Thus in none of the relevant senses of "responsible" can determinism entail that no one is ever responsible. The Argument from Determinism would then seem to fail.

In conclusion I mention one further reason why it has for so long been thought that determinism and responsibility are incompatible. The advance of some sciences, particularly psychology, economics, and sociology really has brought to light many alarming facts about inadequate upbringing, ignorance among wide sections of the population of the prevailing obligatory requirements, and the nature of their justification, not to mention the frequent injustice and even viciousness of these requirements. All of this has cast considerable doubt on the justifiability of regarding and treating people as culpable whenever they fail to satisfy such requirements. Many sincere reformers, impressed by these specific arguments based on empirical investigations of the conditions under which certain individuals and groups live, are then prone to embrace general conclusions about culpability based on general nonempirical premises about determinism. But this can only weaken their deserving case.

THE MENTAL HEALTH ETHIC

Thomas S. Szasz, M.D.

THOMAS S. SZASZ, M.D., is Professor of Psychiatry at the State University of New York in Syracuse. He has also taught at the Chicago Institute for Psychoanalysis and at the University of Wisconsin. In addition to technical papers on psychiatry he has written on the civil rights of mental patients, criminal responsibility, civil liberties, morals and psychiatry, and politics and mental health. He is the author of *Pain and Pleasure* (1957), *The Myth of Mental Illness* (1961), *Law, Liberty, and Psychiatry* (1963), *The Ethics of Psychoanalysis* (1965), and *Psychiatric Justice* (1965).

INTRODUCTION

If it is true, as Sartre says, that while "one speaks in one's own language, one writes in a foreign language,"[1] the risk of using words in imprecise, incorrect, or misleading ways is at once grave and widespread.

Yet communicate we must. And if we do not communicate in the unambiguous language of mathematics, we must try to make our everyday language clear. Let me begin, therefore, with some comments about the meaning of "ethics," "psychiatry," and related terms.

Webster's Third New International Dictionary (unabridged), defines ethics as "the discipline dealing with what is good and bad or right and wrong or with moral duty and

[1] J. P. Sartre, *The Words*, Bernard Frechtman, trans. (New York, 1964), p. 164.

85

obligation . . ."; also as "a group of moral principles or set of values . . ."; and finally, as "the principles of conduct governing an individual or a profession . . . standards of behavior . . ."

Ethics is a distinctly human affair. There are "principles of conduct" governing individuals and groups, but there are no such principles governing the behavior of animals, machines, or stars. Indeed, the word "conduct" implies this: only persons *conduct* themselves; animals *behave*, machines *function*, and stars *move*.

Is it too much to say, then, that any human behavior that constitutes conduct—which, in other words, is a product of choice or potential choice, and not simply of a reflex—is, *ipso facto*, moral conduct? In all such conduct, considerations of good and bad, or right and wrong, play a role. Logically, its study belongs in the domain of ethics. The ethicist is a behavioral scientist par excellence.

If we examine the definition and practice of psychiatry, however, we find that in many ways it is a covert redefinition of the nature and scope of ethics. According to Webster's, psychiatry is "a branch of medicine that deals with the science and practice of treating mental, emotional, or behavioral disorders, especially as originating in endogenous causes or resulting from faulty interpersonal relationships"; further, it is "a treatise or text on or theory of the etiology, recognition, treatment, or prevention of mental, emotional, or behavioral disorder, or the application of psychiatric principles to any area of human activity (social psychiatry)"; thirdly, it is "the psychiatric service in a general hospital (this patient should be referred to psychiatry)."

The nominal aim of psychiatry is the study and treatment of mental disorders. But what are mental disorders? To accept the existence of a class of phenomena called "mental diseases," rather than to inquire into the conditions under which some persons may designate others as "mentally ill," is the decisive step in the embracing of the mental health ethic.[2] If we take the dictionary definition of this discipline seriously, the study of a large part of human behavior is subtly transferred from ethics to psychiatry. For while the ethicist is supposedly concerned only with normal (moral) behavior, and the psychiatrist only with abnormal (emotionally disordered) behavior, the very distinction between the two rests on ethical grounds. In other words, the assertion that a person is mentally ill involves rendering a moral judgment about him. Moreover, because of the social consequences of such a judgment, both the "mental patient" and those who treat him as one become actors in a morality play, albeit in one written in a medical-psychiatric jargon.

Having removed mentally disordered behavior from the purview of the ethicist, the psychiatrist has had to justify his reclassification. He has done so by redefining the *quality* or *nature* of the behavior he studies: whereas the ethicist studies moral behavior, the psychiatrist studies biological or mechanical behavior. In Webster's words, the psychiatrist's concern is with behavior "originating in endogenous causes or resulting from faulty interpersonal relationships." We should fasten our attention here on the words "causes" and "resulting." With these words, the transition from ethics to physiology, and hence to medicine and psychiatry, is securely completed.

Ethics is meaningful only in a context of self-governing individuals or groups exercising more or less free, uncoerced choices. Conduct resulting from such choices is said to have reasons and meanings, but no causes. This is the well-known polarity between determinism and voluntarism, causality and free will, natural science and moral science.

Defining psychiatry in the above way leads not only to a reapportionment of disciplines taught in universities, but also promotes a point of view about the nature of some types of human behavior, and about man in general.

[2] See my books *The Myth of Mental Illness: Foundations of a Theory of Personal Conduct* (New York, 1961) and *Law, Liberty and Psychiatry: An Inquiry into the Social Uses of Mental Health Practices* (New York, 1963).

By assigning "endogenous causes" to human behavior, such behavior is classified as *happening*, rather than as *action*. Diabetes mellitus is a disease caused by an endogenous lack of enzymes necessary to metabolize carbohydrates. In this frame of reference, the endogenous cause of a depression must be either a metabolic defect (that is, an antecedent chemical event), or a defect in "interpersonal relationships" (that is, an antecedent historical event). Future events or expectations are excluded as possible "causes" of a feeling of depression. Yet, is this reasonable? Consider the millionaire who finds himself financially ruined because of business reverses. How shall we explain his "depression" (if we so want to label his feeling of dejection)? By regarding it as the *result* of the events mentioned, and perhaps of others in his childhood? Or as the *expression* of his view of himself and of his powers in the world, present and future? To choose the former is to redefine ethical conduct as psychiatric malady.

The healing arts—especially medicine, religion, and psychiatry—operate within society, not outside it. Indeed, they are an important part of society. It is not surprising, therefore, that these institutions reflect and promote the primary moral values of the community. Moreover, today, as in the past, one or another of these institutions is used to *mold* society by supporting certain values and opposing others. What is the role of psychiatry in promoting a covert system of ethics in contemporary American society? What are the moral values it espouses and imposes on society? I shall try to suggest some answers by examining the position of certain representative psychiatric works and by making explicit the nature of the mental health ethic. I shall try to show that in the dialogue between the two major ideologies of our day—individualism and collectivism—the mental health ethic comes down squarely on the side of collectivism.

THE INDIVIDUAL AND HIS ENEMIES

Men desire freedom and fear it. Karl R. Popper speaks of the "enemies of the open society,"[3] and Erich Fromm of those who "escape from freedom."[4] Craving liberty and self-determination, men desire to stand alone as individuals; but, fearing loneliness and responsibility, they wish also to unite with their fellow men as members of a group.

Theoretically, individualism and collectivism are antagonistic principles: for the former, the supreme values are personal autonomy and individual liberty, for the latter, solidarity with the group and collective security. Practically, the antagonism is only partial: man needs to be both—alone, as a solitary individual, and with his fellow man, as a member of a group. Thoreau at Walden Pond and the man in the gray flannel suit in his bureaucratic organization are two ends of a spectrum: most men seek to steer a course between these extremes. Individualism and collectivism may thus be pictured as the two shores of a fast-moving river, between which we—as moral men—must navigate. The careful, the timid, and perhaps the "wise" will take the middle course: like the practical politician, such a person will seek accommodation to "social reality" by affirming and denying both individualism and collectivism.

Although, in general, an ethical system which values individualism will be hostile to one which values collectivism, and vice versa, an important difference between the two must be noted. In an individualistic society, men are not prevented by force from forming voluntary associations, nor are they punished for assuming submissive roles in groups. In contrast, in a collectivistic society, men are prevented by force from abstaining from participation in certain organizational activities, and are punished for pursuing a solitary and independent

[3] *The Open Society and Its Enemies* (Princeton, 1950).
[4] *Escape from Freedom* (New York, 1941).

existence. The reason for this difference is simple: as a social ethic, individualism seeks to minimize coercion and fosters the development of a pluralistic society; whereas collectivism regards coercion as a necessary means for achieving desired ends and fosters the development of a singularistic society.

The collectivist ethic is exemplified in the Soviet Union, as in the case of Iosif Brodsky. A twenty-four-year-old Jewish poet, Brodsky was brought to trial in Leningrad for "pursuing a parasitic way of life." This charge stems from "a Soviet legal concept that was enacted into law in 1961 to permit the exiling of city residents not performing 'socially useful labor.'"[5]

Brodsky had two hearings, the first on February 18, the second on March 13. The transcript of the trial was smuggled out of Russia, and its translation published in *The New Leader*.[6] In the first hearing Brodsky was vaguely accused of being a poet and of not doing more "productive" work. At its conclusion, the judge ordered Brodsky to be sent "for an official psychiatric examination during which it will be determined whether Brodsky is suffering from some sort of psychological illness or not and whether this illness will prevent Brodsky from being sent to a distant locality for forced labor. Taking into consideration that from the history of his illness it is apparent that Brodsky has evaded hospitalization, it is hereby ordered that division No. 18 of the militia be in charge of bringing him to the official psychiatric examination."

This point of view is characteristic of the collectivist ethic. It is also indistinguishable from that of contemporary American institutional psychiatry. In both systems, a person who has harmed no one but is considered "deviant" is defined as mentally ill; he is ordered to submit to psychiatric examination; if he resists, this is viewed as a further sign of his mental abnormality.

Brodsky was found guilty and sent "to a distant locality

[5] *The New York Times* (August 31, 1964), 8.
[6] "The Trial of Iosif Brodsky: A Transcript," *The New Leader*, Vol. 47, No. 18, August 31, 1964, 6–17.

for a period of five years of enforced labor." His sentence, it should be noted, was at once therapeutic, in that it sought to promote Brodsky's "personal well-being," and penal, in that it sought to punish him for the harm he inflicted on the community. This, too, is the classic collectivist thesis: what is good for the community, is good for the individual. Since the individual is denied any existence apart from the group, this equation of the one with the many is quite logical.

Another Russian man of letters, Valeriy Tarsis, who had published a book in England describing the predicament of writers and intellectuals under the Khrushchev regime, was incarcerated in a mental hospital in Moscow. It may be recalled that the American poet Ezra Pound had been dealt with in the same way: he was incarcerated in a mental hospital in Washington, D.C. In his autobiographical novel, *Ward 7*, Tarsis gives the impression that involuntary mental hospitalization is a widely used Soviet technique for repressing social deviance.[7]

It seems clear that the enemy of the Soviet state is not the capitalist entrepreneur, but the lonely worker—not the Rockefellers, but the Thoreaus. In the religion of collectivism, heresy is individualism: the outcast par excellence is the person who refuses to be a member of the team.

I shall argue that the main thrust of contemporary American psychiatry—as exemplified by so-called community psychiatry—is toward the creation of a collectivist society, with all this implies for economic policy, personal liberty, and social conformity.

COMMUNITY PSYCHIATRY

If by "community psychiatry" we mean mental health care provided by the community through public funds—rather than by the individual or by voluntary groups through private

[7] See Valeriy Tarsis, *Ward 7: An Autobiographical Novel*, Katya Brown, trans. (London and Glasgow, 1965).

funds—then community psychiatry is as old as American psychiatry. (In most other countries, too, psychiatry began as a community enterprise and never ceased to function in that role.)

Fresh as the term "community psychiatry" is, many psychiatrists freely admit that it is just another slogan in the profession's unremitting campaign to sell itself to the public. At the fourth annual meeting of the Association of Medical Superintendents of Mental Hospitals, the main topic was community psychiatry—"What it is and what it isn't."[8] "What is community psychiatry?" asked the director of an eastern state hospital. His answer: "I went to two European congresses this summer and I don't know what is meant by the term. . . . When people talk about it, it is rarely clear what it is." To a psychiatrist in a midwestern state, "Community psychiatry . . . means that we collaborate within the framework of existing medical and psychiatric facilities." This view was supported by a psychiatrist from an eastern state hospital, who asserted that "In Pennsylvania, the state hospitals are already serving the communities in which they are located. . . . They have been carrying out community psychiatry." Such is the path of progress in psychiatry.

What I found particularly disturbing in this report was that, although many who attended the meeting were uncertain about what community psychiatry is or might be, all declared their firm intention to play a leading role in it. Said a psychiatrist from a midwestern state hospital: "What community psychiatry is, whatever it becomes, we'd better have a part in it. We'd better assume leadership or we will get the part relegated to us. We should be functioning as community mental hospitals. If we sit back and say we are not community mental health centers, we will have a great many people telling us what to do." The President of the medical superintendents' organization then called upon the members to

[8] Roche Report, "Community Psychiatry and Mental Hospitals," *Frontiers of Hospital Psychiatry*, Vol. 1, No. 16 (November 15, 1964), 1, 2, and 9.

"assume a role of leadership." There was general agreement on this: "Unless we participate and take a dominant part, we will be relegated to the bottom of the heap," warned a psychiatrist from a midwestern state hospital.

If this is community psychiatry, what is new about it? Why is it praised and recommended as if it were some novel medical advance which promises to revolutionize the "treatment" of the "mentally ill"? To answer these questions would require an historical study of our subject, which I shall not attempt here. Let it suffice to note the specific forces that launched community psychiatry as a discrete movement or discipline. These forces are of two kinds—one political, the other psychiatric.

The social policies of modern interventionist liberalism, launched by Franklin D. Roosevelt in this country, received powerful reinforcement during the presidency of John F. Kennedy. President Kennedy's Message to Congress on "Mental Illness and Mental Retardation" on February 5, 1963, reflects this spirit. Although the care of the hospitalized mentally ill has been traditionally a welfare-state operation—carried out through the facilities of the various State Departments of Mental Hygiene and the Veterans Administration—he advocated an even broader program, supported by public funds. Said the President: "I propose a national mental health program to assist in the inauguration of a wholly new emphasis and approach to care for the mentally ill . . . Government at every level—federal, state, and local—private foundations and individual citizens must all face up to their responsibilities in this area."[9]

Gerald Caplan, whose book Robert Felix called the "Bible . . . of the community mental health worker," hailed this message as "the first official pronouncement on this topic by the head of a government in this or any other country."

[9] John F. Kennedy, "Message from the President of the United States Relative to Mental Illness and Mental Retardation." (U.S. 88th Congress, First Session, 1963 House of Representatives. Document no. 58, p. 2.)

Henceforward, he added, "the prevention, treatment, and rehabilitation of the mentally ill and the mentally retarded are to be considered a community responsibility and not a private problem to be dealt with by individuals and their families in consultation with their medical advisers."[10]

Without clearly defining what community psychiatry *is,* or what it can or will *do,* the enterprise is proclaimed good merely because it is a team effort, involving the community and the government, and not a personal effort, involving individuals and their voluntary associations. We are told that the promotion of "community mental health" is so complex a problem that it requires the intervention of the government—but that the individual citizen is responsible for its success.

Community psychiatry is barely off the drawing board; its nature and achievements are but high-flowing phrases and utopian promises. Indeed, perhaps the only thing clear about it is its hostility to the psychiatrist in private practice who ministers to the individual patient: he is depicted as one engaged in a nefarious activity. His role has more than a slight similarity to that of Brodsky, the parasite-poet of Leningrad. Michael Gorman, for example, quotes approvingly Henry Brosin's reflections about the social role of the psychiatrist: "There is no question that the challenge of the role of psychiatry is with us all the time. The interesting thing is what we will be like in the future. Not the stereotypes and strawmen of the old AMA private entrepreneurs."[11]

I have cited the views of some of the propagandists of community psychiatry. But what about the work itself? Its main goal seems to be the dissemination of a collectivistic mental health ethic, as a kind of secular religion. I shall support this view by quotations from the leading textbook of community psychiatry, the *Principles of Preventive Psychiatry* by Gerald Caplan.

[10] Gerald Caplan, *Principles of Preventive Psychiatry* (New York, 1964), p. 3.

[11] "Psychiatry and Public Policy," *American Journal of Psychiatry,* 122: 55–60, 1965.

What Caplan describes is a system of bureaucratic psychiatry in which more and more psychiatrists do less and less actual work with so-called patients. The community psychiatrist's principal role is to be a "mental health consultant": this means that he talks to people, who talk to other people, and finally someone talks to, or has some sort of contact with, someone who is considered actually or potentially "mentally ill." This scheme works in conformity with Parkinson's Law:[12] the expert at the top of the pyramid is so important and so "busy" that he needs a huge army of subordinates to help him; and his subordinates need a huge army of second-order subordinates; and so on. In a society faced with large-scale unemployment due to automation and great technological advances, the prospect of a "preventive" mental health industry, ready and able to absorb a vast amount of manpower should be politically attractive indeed. It is. (More about this later.) Let us now look more closely at this aspect of the work of the community psychiatrist.

According to Caplan, a main task of the community psychiatrist is to provide more and better "sociocultural supplies" to people. It is not clear what these supplies are. For example, "the mental health specialist" is described as someone who "offers consultation to legislators and administrators and collaborates with other citizens in influencing governmental agencies to change laws and regulations."[13] In plain English, a lobbyist for the mental health bureaucracy.

The community psychiatrist also helps "the legislators and welfare authorities improve the moral atmosphere in the homes where [illegitimate] children are being brought up and to influence their mothers to marry and provide them with stable fathers."[14] Although Caplan mentions the community psychiatrist's concern with the effects of divorce upon

[12] See C. N. Parkinson, *Parkinson's Law and Other Studies in Administration* (New York, 1962).
[13] Caplan, *op. cit.*, p. 56.
[14] *Ibid.*, p. 59.

children, there is no comment about advising women who want help in securing divorces, abortions, or contraceptives.

Another function of the mental health specialist is to review "the conditions of life of his target group in the population and then influence(s) those who help to determine these conditions so that their laws, regulations, and policies . . . are modified in an appropriate direction."[15] Caplan emphasizes that he is not advocating government by psychiatrists; he is aware that the psychiatrist may thus become the agent or spokesman of certain political or social groups. He disposes of the problem by declaring that every psychiatrist must make this decision for himself, and that his book is not addressed to those who wish to provide services for special interest groups, but rather to "those who direct their efforts primarily to the reduction of mental disorder in our communities."[16] But he admits that the distinction between psychiatrists who exploit their professional knowledge in the service of an organization and "those who work in the organization in order to achieve the goals of their profession" is not that simple in practice. For example, commenting on the role of consulting psychiatrists in the Peace Corps, he blandly observes that their success "is not unassociated with the fact that they were able to wholeheartedly accept the major goals of that organization, and their enthusiasm was quickly perceived by its leaders."[17] But there is no satisfactory answer to the dangers posed by an excess of "enthusiasm" on the part of a naïve or unscrupulous psychiatrist in such a position.

On the psychiatrist's proper role in the medical clinics of his community (specifically in relation to his function in a baby clinic, seeing a mother who has a "disturbed" relationship with her child), Caplan writes: "If the preventive psychiatrist can convince the medical authorities in the clinics that his operations are a logical extension of traditional medical practice, his role will be sanctioned by all concerned, in-

[15] Caplan, *op. cit.*, pp. 62–63.
[16] *Ibid.*, p. 65.
[17] *Ibid.*

cluding himself. All that remains for him to do is to work out the technical details."[18]

But this is precisely what I regard as the central question: Is so-called mental health work "a logical extension of traditional medical practice," either preventive or curative? I say it is not a logical but a rhetorical extension of it.[19] In other words, the practice of mental health education and community psychiatry is not medical practice, but moral suasion and political coercion.

THE MENTAL HEALTH ETHIC

Mental health and illness are but new words for describing moral values. More generally, the semantics of the mental health movement is but a new vocabulary for promoting a particular kind of secular ethic.

This view may be supported in several ways. Here I shall try to do so by citing the opinions expressed by the Scientific Committee of the World Federation for Mental Health in the monograph, *Mental Health and Value Systems,* edited by Kenneth Soddy.

In the first chapter, the authors candidly acknowledge "that mental health is associated with principles dependent upon the prevailing religion or ideology of the community concerned."[20]

There then follows a review of the various concepts of mental health proposed by different workers. For example, in Soddy's opinion, "A healthy person's response to life is without strain; his ambitions are within the scope of practical

[18] *Ibid.,* p. 79.
[19] See my book *The Myth of Mental Illness: Foundations of a Theory of Personal Conduct* and my article "The Moral Dilemma of Psychiatry: Autonomy or Heteronomy?" in the *American Journal of Psychiatry,* 121: 521–28, 1964.
[20] *Cross-Cultural Studies in Mental Health: Identity* [and] *Mental Health and Value Systems* (Chicago, 1962), p. 70.

realization. . . ."[21] For O'Doherty, mental health "demands good interpersonal relations with oneself, with others, and with God"[22]—a definition that would neatly place all atheists in the class of the mentally sick.

The authors consider the vexing problem of the relation between social adaptation and mental health. They succeed admirably in evading the problem which they claim to be tackling: "mental health and social adaptation are not identical . . . (this) can be illustrated by the fact that few people would regard a person who had become better adjusted as a result of leaving home and moving into a different society as having thereby become mentally healthy. . . . In the past, and still today in some societies, adaptation to society has tended to be highly valued . . . as a sign of mental health; and failure to adapt has been even more strongly regarded as a sign of mental ill-health. . . . There are occasions and situations in which, from the point of view of mental health, rebellion and non-conformity may be far more important than social adaptation."[23] No criteria are given for distinguishing, "from the point of view of mental health," the situations to which we ought to conform from those against which we ought to rebel.

There is much more of this kind of sanctimonious foolishness. Thus, we are told that "While it is unlikely that agreement could be reached on the proposition that all 'bad' people are mentally unhealthy, it might be possible to agree that no 'bad' person could be said to have the highest possible level of mental health, and that many 'bad' people are mentally unhealthy."[24] But the problems of who is to decide who the "bad" people are, and by what means they are to decide, are glossed over. This evasion of the reality of conflicting ethics in the world as it exists is the most outstanding feature of this study. Perhaps one of the aims of propounding

[21] *Cross-Cultural Studies* . . . , p. 72.
[22] *Ibid.*, p. 73.
[23] *Ibid.*, pp. 75–76.
[24] *Ibid.*, p. 82.

a fuzzy, yet comprehensive, mental health ethic is to maintain this denial. Indeed, the true goal of the community psychiatrist seems to be to replace a clear political vocabulary with an obscure psychiatric semantic, and a pluralistic system of moral values with a singularistic mental health ethic. Here is an example of the way this is accomplished.

"Our view is that the assumption of an attitude of superiority by one social group towards another is not conducive to the mental health of either group."[25] Some simplistic comments about the Negro problem in America then follow. No doubt, the sentiment here expressed is admirable. But the real problems of psychiatry are bound up not with abstract groups but with concrete individuals. Yet nothing is said about actual relations between people—for example, between adults and children, doctors and patients, experts and clients; and how, in these various situations, the attainment of a relationship that is both egalitarian and functional requires the utmost skill and effort of all concerned (and may, in some cases, be impossible to realize).

Self-revealing as the mental health ethicist is when he discusses mental health and illness, his moral stance is even clearer when he discusses psychiatric treatment. Indeed, the promoter of mental health now emerges as a social engineer on the grand scale: he will be satisfied with nothing less than gaining license to export his own ideology to a world market.

The authors begin their discussion of the promotion of mental health by noting the "resistances" against it: "The principles underlying success in attempts to alter cultural conditions *in the interest of mental health,* and the hazards of such attempts, are very important considerations for practical mental health work. . . . The introduction of change in a community may be subject to conditions not unlike those which obtain in the case of *the child* . . . [my emphasis]."[26] We recognize here the familiar medical-psychiatric model of

25 *Ibid.,* p. 106.
26 *Ibid.,* p. 173.

human relations: the client is like the ignorant child who must be "protected," if need be autocratically and without his consent, by the expert who is like the omnicompetent parent.

The mental health worker who subscribes to this point of view and engages in this kind of work adopts a condescending attitude toward his (unwilling) clients: he regards them, at best, as stupid children in need of education, and, at worst, as evil criminals in need of correction. All too often he seeks to impose value-change through fraud and force, rather than through truth and example. In brief, he does not practice what he preaches. The egalitarian-loving attitude toward one's fellow man, which the mental health worker is so eager to export to the "psychiatrically underdeveloped" areas of the world, seems to be in rather short supply everywhere. Or are we to overlook the relations in the United States between white and black, or psychiatrist and involuntary patient?

The authors are not wholly oblivious of these difficulties. But they seem to think it sufficient to acknowledge their awareness of such problems. For example, after commenting on the similarities between Chinese brainwashing and involuntary psychiatric treatment, they write:

"The term brain-washing has . . . been applied with unfortunate connotations to psychotherapeutic practice *by those who are hostile to it*. We consider that the lesson of this needs to be taken to heart by all who are responsible for securing psychiatric treatment of non-volitional patients. The use of compulsion or deceit will almost certainly *appear to those who are unfriendly to or frightened of* the aims of psychotherapy, to be wicked [my emphasis]."[27]

The "benevolent" despot, whether political or psychiatric, does not like to have his benevolence questioned. If it is, he resorts to the classic tactic of the oppressor: he tries to silence his critic, and, if this fails, he tries to degrade him. The psychiatrist accomplishes this by calling those who disagree with him "hostile" or "mentally ill." Here we are told that if a

[27] *Cross-Cultural Studies . . . ,* p. 186.

person admits to the similarities between brainwashing and involuntary psychiatric treatment he is, *ipso facto, hostile* to psychotherapy.

The statement about "the lesson . . . to be taken to heart by all who are *responsible* for securing psychiatric treatment of non-volitional patients [emphasis added]" requires special comment. The language used implies that involuntary mental patients exist in nature—whereas, in fact, they are created, partly by psychiatrists. Thus, after raising the vexing problem of involuntary psychiatric treatment, the authors fail to deal with it in a clear and forthright manner; instead, they impugn the emotional health and moral intentions of those who would dare to look at the problem critically.

This antagonism to a critical examination of his doctrines and methods may be necessary for the mental health worker, just as it is for the missionary or the politician: the aim of each is to conquer souls or minds, not to understand human problems. Let us not forget the dangers of trying to understand another person: the effort invites disproof of one's views and questioning of one's beliefs. The thoughtful person who is content to teach by the example of his own conduct must always be ready to acknowledge error and to change his ways. But this is not what the mental health worker wants: he does not want to change his ways, but those of others.

In an analysis of the mental hygiene movement written nearly thirty years ago, Kingsley Davis has suggested this and more. Commenting on the "family clinic," Davis observed that such agencies offer not medical treatment but moral manipulation: "Before one can cure such patients, one must alter their purpose; in short, one must operate, not on their anatomy, but on their system of values."[28] The trouble is, of course, that people usually do not want to alter their goals— they want to attain them. As a result, "Only those clients whose ends correspond to socially sanctioned values may be

[28] "The Application of Science to Personal Relations: A Critique of the Family Clinic Idea," *American Sociological Review,* 1: 238, 1936.

expected to come voluntarily to such a clinic. Other troubled persons whose wishes are opposed to accepted values, will stay away; they can be brought in only through force or fraud."[29] Nor does Davis shirk from stating what many know but few dare articulate—namely, that "many clients are lured to family clinics by misrepresentation."[30] Similarly, many more are lured to state mental hospitals and community-sponsored clinics. Community psychiatry thus emerges, in my opinion at least, as a fresh attempt to revitalize and expand the old mental hygiene industry.

First, there is a new advertising campaign: mental health education is an effort to lure unsuspecting persons into becoming clients of the community mental health services. Then, having created a demand—or, in this case, perhaps merely the appearance of one—the industry expands: this takes the form of steadily increasing expenditures for existing mental hospitals and clinics and for creating new, more highly automated factories, called "community mental health centers."

Before concluding this review of the ethics of mental health work, I want to comment briefly on the values advocated by the authors of *Mental Health and Value Systems*.

They promote change as such; its direction is often left unspecified. "The success of mental health promotion depends partly upon the creation of a climate favourable to change and a belief that change is desirable and possible."[31] They also emphasize the need to scrutinize certain "unproven assumptions": none of these, however, pertains to the nature of mental health work. Instead, they list as unproven assumptions such ideas as "that the mother is always the best person to have charge of her own child."[32]

I believe that we ought to object to all this on basic logical and moral grounds: if moral values are to be discussed and

[29] Davis, *loc. cit.*, 241.
[30] *Ibid.*
[31] *Op. cit.*, p. 209.
[32] *Ibid.*, p. 208.

promoted, they ought to be considered for what they are—moral values, not health values. Why? Because moral values are, and must be, the legitimate concern of everyone and fall under the special competence of no particular group; whereas health values (and especially their technical implementation) are, and must be, the concern mainly of experts on health, especially physicians.

ECONOMICS, MENTAL HEALTH, AND SOCIETY

Regardless of what we call it, mental health today is a big business. This is true in every modern society, whatever its political structure. It is impossible, therefore, to comprehend the struggle between individualistic and collectivistic values in psychiatry without a clear understanding of the social organization of mental health care.

Surprising as it may seem, in the United States, 98 per cent of the care for the hospitalized mentally ill is provided by federal, state, and county governments.[33] The situation in Great Britain is similar. In the Soviet Union the figure is 100 per cent.

To be sure, this is not the whole picture for the United States or Great Britain. Private practice is still what the term implies: private. Yet this does not mean that psychiatric inpatient care is paid for by public funds and psychiatric outpatient care by private funds. Outpatient services are financed both privately and publicly. Including all types of care, it has been estimated that "about 65% of the treatment of mental patients goes on in tax supported services, and 35% in private and voluntary services."[34]

The implications of the vast and expanding involvement of the government in mental health care have, I think, been in-

---

[33] Daniel Blain, "Action in Mental Health: Opportunities and Responsibilities of the Private Sector of Society," *American Journal of Psychiatry*, 121: 425, 1964.
[34] *Ibid.*

sufficiently appreciated. Moreover, whatever problems stem from government control of mental hospital care, these difficulties are connected with a logically antecedent problem: What is the aim of the care provided? It does not help to say that it is to transform the mentally sick into the mentally healthy. We have seen that the terms "mental health" and "mental sickness" designate ethical values and social performances. The mental hospital system thus serves, however covertly, to promote certain values and performances, and to suppress others. Which values are promoted and which suppressed depends, of course, on the nature of the society sponsoring the "health" care.

Again, these points are not new. Similar views have been voiced by others. Davis observed that the prospective clients of family clinics "are told in one way or another, through lectures, newspaper publicity, or discreet announcement, that the clinic exists for the purpose of helping individuals out of their troubles; whereas it really exists for the purpose of helping the established social order. Once lured to the clinic, the individual may suffer further deception in the form of propaganda to the effect that his own best interest lies in doing the thing he apparently does not want to do, as if a man's 'best interest' could be judged by anything else than his own desires."[35]

Because of the involuntary character of this kind of clinic or hospital, it follows, according to Davis (and I agree with him), that the service "must find support through subsidy (philanthropic or governmental) rather than through profit from fees. Furthermore, since its purpose is identified with the community at large rather than the persons it serves, and since it requires the use of force or misrepresentation to carry out this purpose, it must function as an arm of the law and government. We do not permit the use of force and fraud to individuals in their private capacity . . . In order, therefore, to settle familial conflicts by enforcing social dictates, a

[35] Davis, *loc. cit.*, 241–42.

family clinic must in the long run be clothed with the power or at least the mantle of some state-authorized institution for the exercise of systematic deception, such as the church."[36]

Could the community support a clinic devoted to promoting the best interests of the client, rather than of the community? Davis considered this possibility, and concluded that it could not. For, if this kind of clinic is to exist, then, "like the other kind, (it) must use force and deception—not on the client, but on the community. It must lobby in legislative halls, employ political weapons, and above all deny publicly its true purpose."[37] (We have seen organized American psychoanalysis do just this.)[38]

Davis is clear about the basic alternatives which psychiatry must face, but which it refuses to face: "The individualistic clinic would accept the standard of its client. The other kind of clinic would accept the standard of society. In practice only the latter is acceptable, because the state is clothed with the power to use force and fraud."[39] Insofar as family clinics or other kinds of mental health facilities try to render services of both kinds, "they are trying to ride two horses headed in opposite directions."[40]

Comparison of the care provided by mental hospitals in Russia and America supports the contention that the values and performances which psychiatry promotes or suppresses are related to the society sponsoring the psychiatric service. The proportion of physicians and hospital beds to population is about the same in both countries. However, this similarity is misleading. In the Soviet Union, there are about 200,000 psychiatric hospital beds; in the United States about 750,000.

[36] Davis, *loc. cit.*, 242–43.

[37] *Ibid.*, 243.

[38] See my articles "Psychoanalysis and Taxation: A Contribution to the Rhetoric of the Disease Concept in Psychiatry," in the *American Journal of Psychotherapy*, 18: 635–43, 1964, and "A Note on Psychiatric Rhetoric," in the *American Journal of Psychiatry*, 121: 1192–93, 1965.

[39] Davis, *loc. cit.*, 244.

[40] *Ibid.*, 245.

Accordingly, "11.2% of all hospital beds in the Soviet Union (are) allocated to psychiatric patients compared with 46.4% in the USA."[41]

This difference is best accounted for by certain social and psychiatric policies which encourage mental hospitalization in America, but discourage it in Russia. Moreover, the Soviet's main emphasis in psychiatric care is enforced work, whereas ours is enforced idleness; they compel psychiatric patients to produce, whereas we compel them to consume. It seems improbable that these "therapeutic" emphases should be unrelated to the chronic labor shortage in Russia, and the chronic surplus here.

In Russia, "work therapy" differs from plain work in that the former is carried out under the auspices of a psychiatric institution, the latter under the auspices of a factory or farm. Furthermore, as we saw in the case of Iosif Brodsky, the Russian criminal is sentenced to work—not to idleness (or makework), like his American counterpart. All this stems from two basic sources: first, from the Soviet social-political theory which holds that "productive work" is necessary and good for both society and the individual; second, from the Soviet socioeconomic fact that in a system of mammoth bureaucracies (lacking adequate checks and balances) more and more people are needed to do less and less work. Thus, the Soviets have a chronic labor shortage.

Consistent with these conditions, the Russians try to keep people at their jobs, rather than put them in mental hospitals. If a person is no longer tolerated at his job, he is made to work in "psychiatric outpatient clinics . . . where patients (can) spend the entire day at work. . . ."[42] In the 1930s, during the heyday of Stalinism, there developed an "uncritical infatuation with work therapy" as a result of which "the hospital came to resemble industrial plants."[43]

[41] J. Wortis and D. Freundlich, "Psychiatric Work Therapy in the Soviet Union," *American Journal of Psychiatry*, 121: 123, 1964.
[42] *Ibid.*
[43] *Ibid.*, 124.

It is evident that the distinction, in Russia, between work therapy and plain work is of the same kind as the distinction, in the United States, between confinement in a hospital for the criminally insane and imprisonment in jail.[44] Many of the Soviet hospital shops, we learn, "settle down to operate like regular factory units, keeping their mildly disabled but productive patients there for interminable periods, paying them regular wages while they travel daily back and forth to their homes as if they had permanent jobs. . . . Instances have been reported where the sheltered workshops have been exploited by their managers for private gain. . . ."[45]

In the United States, the government does not usually own or control the means of production. The manufacture of goods, and the provision of (most) services, is in the hands of private individuals or groups. If the government should want or need persons under its care to produce goods or provide services, it would create a problem of competition with private enterprise. This problem first arose in connection with prisons and now faces us in connection with mental health facilities. The stockholders of General Motors Corporation (or its employees) would be less than happy if the United States Government were to have the inmates of federal prisons manufacture automobiles. Thus, prisoners in America are reduced to making license plates, and mental patients, to mopping floors or working in the kitchen or back ward of the hospital.

The point I wish to make is simple: unlike in Russia, the major socioeconomic problem in the United States is an overabundance, not a scarcity, of consumer goods; likewise, we have an excess, not a shortage, of productive manpower. The result is our well-known chronic unemployment, which rarely dips below 5 per cent of the labor force (without including

[44] See my books *Law, Liberty, and Psychiatry: An Inquiry into the Social Uses of Mental Health Practices* and *Psychiatric Justice* (New York, 1965).

[45] Wortis and Freundlich, *loc. cit.*, 127.

many elderly persons capable of working). Accordingly, in American mental hospitals, meaningful and productive work is discouraged and, if need be, prevented by force. Instead of defining forced labor as therapy, as do the Soviets—we define forced idleness as therapy. The only work permitted (or encouraged) is labor necessary to maintain the hospital plant and services, and even in this category only such work as is considered non-competitive with private enterprise.

As I suggested some time ago,[46] in the United States mental hospitalization serves a two-fold socioeconomic function. (To what extent the functions of such hospitalization also constitute its aims is difficult to ascertain.) First, by defining people in mental hospitals as unfit for work (and often preventing them from working even after their discharge), the mental health care system serves to diminish our national pool of unemployment: large numbers of people are classified as mentally ill, rather than as socially incompetent or unemployed. Second, by creating a vast organization of psychiatric hospitals and affiliated institutions, the mental health care system helps to provide employment: indeed, the number of psychiatric and parapsychiatric jobs thus created is staggering. As a result, major cutbacks in the expenditures of the mental health bureaucracy threaten the same kind of economic dislocation as do cutbacks in the expenditures of the defense establishment and are, perhaps, equally "unthinkable."

It seems to me, therefore, that contrary to the oftrepeated propaganda about the high cost of mental illness, we have a subtle economic stake in perpetuating, and even increasing, such "illness." Faced as we are with overproduction and underemployment, we can evidently afford the "cost" of caring for hundreds of thousands of mental patients and their dependents. But can we afford the "cost" of not caring for them, and thus adding to the ranks of the unemployed not only the

[46] See my review of Rashi Fein's *Economics of Mental Illness* (New York, 1958), in the *AMA Archives of General Psychiatry*, 1: 116–18, 1959.

so-called mentally ill, but many people who now "treat" them (and do "research" on them)?

Whatever the ostensible aims of community psychiatry may be, its actual operations are likely to be influenced by socioeconomic and political ideas and facts such as I have discussed here.

SUMMARY

Psychiatry is a moral and social enterprise. The psychiatrist deals with problems of human conduct. He is, therefore, drawn into situations of conflict—often between the individual and the group. If we wish to understand psychiatry, we cannot avert our eyes from this dilemma: we must know whose side the psychiatrist takes—the individual's or the group's?

Proponents of the mental health ideology describe the problem in different terms. By not emphasizing conflicts between people, they avoid enlisting themselves explicitly as the agents of either the individual or the group. As they prefer to see it, instead of promoting the interests of one or another party or moral value, they promote "mental health."

Considerations such as these have led me to conclude that the concept of mental illness is a betrayal of common sense and of an ethical view of man. To be sure, whenever we speak of a concept of man, our initial problem is one of definition and philosophy: What do we mean by man? Following in the tradition of individualism and rationalism, I hold that a human being is a person to the extent that he makes free, uncoerced choices. Anything that increases his freedom, increases his manhood; anything that decreases his freedom, decreases his manhood.

Progressive freedom, independence, and responsibility lead to being a man; progressive enslavement, dependence, and irresponsibility, to being a thing. Today it is inescapably clear that, regardless of its origins and aims, the concept of mental illness serves to enslave man. It does so by permitting—indeed commanding—one man to impose his will on another.

We have seen that the purveyors of mental health care, especially when such care is provided by the government, are actually the purveyors of the moral and socioeconomic interests of the state. This is hardly surprising. What other interests could they represent? Surely not those of the so-called patient, whose interests are often antagonistic to those of the state. In this way, psychiatry—now proudly called "community psychiatry"—becomes largely a means for controlling the individual. In a mass society, this is best accomplished by recognizing his existence only as a member of a group, never as an individual.

The danger is clear and has been remarked on by others. In America, when the ideology of totalitarianism is promoted as fascism or communism, it is coldly rejected. However, when the same ideology is promoted under the guise of mental health care, it is warmly embraced. It thus seems possible that where fascism and communism have failed to collectivize American society, the mental health ethic may yet succeed.

RESPECT FOR PERSONS

Errol E. Harris

ERROL E. HARRIS has been Roy Roberts Professor of Philosophy at the University of Kansas since 1962. He has also taught at the University of Witwatersrand, Yale University, Connecticut College, and Edinburgh University. In 1957 he delivered the Terry Lectures at Yale. His published works include *The Survival of Political Man* (1950), *Nature, Mind and Modern Science* (1954), *Revelation through Reason* (1958), and *Foundations of Metaphysics in Science* (1965).

I. INTRODUCTION

When we contemplate our own achievements in the light of the history of civilization, we often find reason for despondency, because in spite of our spectacular and obvious scientific and technical advances we seem to have no similar claim to superiority over past civilizations in politics or in morality. That science and technology have advanced far ahead of anything achieved in past ages the evidence of man-made earth satellites, supersonic airplanes, guided missiles and thermonuclear bombs leaves no room for doubt. But these very products of science and the use to which we put them arouse grave misgivings about our achievements in political organization, in moral insight and practice, or in religious awareness. Our very progress sometimes makes us wish we had lived in earlier and perhaps happier times like the age of Pericles in Athens, Augustus in Rome, or the Italian Renaissance. Yet in this connexion we frequently console ourselves with the reflection that even if the Hebrews developed the

111

most mature religious consciousness, even if the Greeks invented political freedom and constitutional government, and the Romans law and administration, nevertheless they all tolerated slavery, which we have abolished and which we regard as wholly incompatible with adherence to civilized standards. Not even in the New Testament is slavery as a social institution condemned, and Paul sends the slave Onesimus back to Philemon, though, as he says, "no longer as a slave, but as more than a slave—as a dear brother." In this quotation there is significance beyond what meets the eye, and if I were giving a sermon I should use it as a text; but here I am pointing only to the fact that Onesimus is sent back to his master and slavery as an institution at least appears to be condoned. So after all, we may think, we have reason to vaunt ourselves on our moral superiority, because we neither practice nor condone slavery and have fought a war to abolish it in our society.

I shall try to show that this boast, if we were to make it, would be based on an illusion and that it is St. Paul in the Epistle who is on higher moral ground, but first I wish to inquire why we consider slavery reprehensible and what we find specially repulsive about it. You may think at once of the abuses of the slave trade, the suffering inflicted on slaves by their captors and the maltreatment of them by the masters who eventually bought them. But clearly this is not all. We should not tolerate slavery today even if we had a guarantee that all slaves would always be humanely treated, for we reject on principle the idea of the sale of human beings like chattels in the open market and their use by others as mere instruments. That indeed is Aristotle's definition of a slave— a living instrument, distinguished from a spade or an axe only by the fact that he is alive, and on a par with domestic animals like the ox or the ass. It is this that we condemn because we believe that human beings should be treated, as Kant maintained, as ends in themselves and never *merely* as means. We censure slavery because it involves the treatment of men as if they were not persons.

From this belief three rules seem to follow as corollaries:

(i) First, that each and every person should be regarded as worthy of sympathetic consideration, and should be so treated;

(ii) Secondly, that no person should be regarded by another as a mere possession; or used as a mere instrument, or treated as a mere obstacle, to another's satisfaction; and

(iii) Thirdly, that persons are not and ought never to be treated in any undertaking as mere expendables.

The moral principle from which these rules derive is what we call "respect for persons." The word "respect" is used here in a special (and almost technical sense). We do not mean that all persons without exception are worthy of the sort of respect that a child owes to his parents or that a pupil gives to a skilled and learned teacher. We do not mean the sentiment appropriate towards moral, intellectual or artistic excellence—though we do mean something akin to this (as it were, its germ or origin). We mean simply that any person, as such, has intrinsic worth or value irrespective of his achievements, which, in the dealings of other persons with him, may be neither ignored nor discounted.

Professor W. G. Maclagan, in a discussion of this principle[1] claims somewhat more for it even than I have done; for two of the rules I have stated are only negative in their import— that persons are not to be treated as instruments or as expendables—and my positive rule is only that everyone has a right to *some* sympathetic consideration. Maclagan asserts that respect for a person implies a positive concern for his welfare independent of the kind of person he may be. It is, he thinks, more than mere justice, which treats all persons impartially, but is compatible with an equal indifference to all of them; it is not simply friendship, for that depends on liking, and the sort of person who is its object; it is not love in the romantic sense, for though that may be blind to faults, it is nevertheless dependent on a peculiar preference as be-

[1] See "Respect for Persons as a Moral Principle," *Philosophy*, XXXV (1960), 193–217.

tween individuals. He identifies it, therefore, with active sympathy coupled with a sense of moral obligation, a duty to be concerned about the welfare of any and every person, for no reason other than that he (or she) is a person and thus has intrinsic worth; and he identifies it as the Christian concept of ἀγάπη. This more positive and exacting account of the principle is, I think, fundamentally sound, and it would follow from the first of my three rules if it were understood as meaning that the sympathetic consideration to which each person was entitled must issue in appropriate action and be commensurate with his status as a potential moral agent—a point on which I shall elaborate further in what follows.

II. QUESTIONS ARISING

From this general statement of what is intended and implied by "respect for persons," three main questions arise. First, if there is a duty to respect persons as such, and without deference to any special relationship we may have with them, or to any special social or ethnic group to which they may belong, what is the source and ground of the obligation? Why should every person, equally with every other, be entitled to my sympathetic consideration?

Secondly, if the source of the duty is the intrinsic worth or value of persons as such, what is this intrinsic value and on what grounds is it ascribed to all persons without distinction?

Thirdly, if we do recognize such an obligation, how do we identify its object? What qualifies a living being as a person? How is personality defined?

The answer to each of these questions is liable to involve the answer to the others. They cannot, therefore, be kept wholly apart and I must crave tolerance of some overlap in what follows.

III. GROUNDS OF OBLIGATION

The first question demands an inquiry into the nature and ground of obligation in general and this obligation in particular.

(1) If I have an obligation to do anything, how does it arise? To be obliged to act in a particular way, is in some sense to be constrained to that act. To act just as I please, on the other hand, is to be free of constraint; so obligation implies some sort of antithesis between what I like and am inclined to do, and what I must or ought to do. This does not necessarily mean that the two can never coincide, but it does mean that inclination is never the source or ground of obligation, and that what one ought to do, one ought to do whether or not one wants to do it. Obligation to act, therefore, is some form of constraint irrespective of inclination.

The question then becomes: Why should I ever be constrained to do what I do not want or am disinclined to do? Now, of course, there are many reasons which spring to mind. I may be threatened by a gangster that if I do not hand over my cash he will shoot me, and this most of us would concede is a form of constraint. But strictly it could be argued that, as I am disinclined to be shot dead by a gangster, my act is still done from inclination or at least the constraint is not independent of inclination—for if I had no objection to being shot, I need not comply. Or again, a policeman, or a system of law enforcement may oblige me, by threat of dire penalties, through minatory messages stuck on the windshield of my car, or by more violent methods, to do things I would rather not do or to refrain from acts I should dearly love to commit. But here also the constraint arises from fear of the penalty and might plausibly be reduced to a stronger inclination. Moral obligation, with which we are concerned, differs from these in that it is a sort of constraint that I recognize in the absence of any threat of punishment or pain to myself. It is an obligation which I impose upon myself even when the consequences of the act may be unpleasant to me and when in other respects I am free to do as I please. So far is it from being done to escape greater pain, that in doing it I may even accept greater pain than I would incur if I followed my inclination. I submit myself to this greater displeasure rather than neglect my duty. It may be that if I neglect a moral obligation I shall feel ashamed of myself and remorseful, but it is not the fear of this that obliges me, for unless I am obliged to do the duty in the first place, my neglect of it will cause me no shame or remorse. Moreover whether or not I do feel shame is up to me. If shame and remorse could be thought of as "punishments," they also would be self-imposed. What, then, can be the ground of this self-imposed obligation?

To give a proper answer to this question I should have to develop a complete ethical theory, and that is beyond the scope of this paper. I must, therefore, resort to brief and dogmatic statements. There are some moral philosophers (known as deontologists) who maintain that we know immediately that certain acts by their very nature are obligatory, without any reference to their consequences, or the good or evil they may entail; but I must confess that I can neither appreciate nor understand any ground for moral obligation which does not derive from something regarded as ultimately and intrinsically good. The source of moral obligation seems to me inevitably to be value, and the object of moral obligation to be the realization of value. If an act is good, I can see why I ought to do it, if not I can not. If there are alternative possibilities, my duty is to do that which is best. I have no other moral obligation. If I ought to keep promises it must be because it is good to do so, if it were not good I ought not to keep them. If there are occasions when I ought to keep a promise, though it seems as if it would be better to break it, this must be because the greater good consequent upon breaking it is only apparent. If it is real, I do not see how I can be obliged to do other than pursue what is really better.

But, of course, I have now only raised another and more fundamental ethical question—What is the criterion of goodness by which we decide which alternative is better? Again I shall have to be brief and dogmatic. From what I have already said about obligation it clearly follows that what is morally good cannot be determined simply by inclination—what I like—because if it were there would be no morality. If there were no difference at all between duty and inclination there would be no moral obligation. But moral obligation is commonly acknowledged, so unless it is pure illusion, goodness must depend on something other than mere desire. Nevertheless, it cannot be quite independent of desire, for what is in no way desirable (whether or not it is actually desired at the moment) cannot be good—rather the contrary.

Human nature being what it is, however, it is not difficult to see how a contrast can arise between what is desired and what is desirable. What I primarily desire is the satisfaction of my natural appetites and needs. But if I seek this without restraint two results occur: (i) my desires come into mutual conflict and (ii) they come into opposition with the desires of other people and lead to conflict with them. If, then, everybody were to give free rein to desire the result would be total frustration and satisfaction would be at a minimum. But man is not simply an appetitive animal and he does not simply seek to satisfy the strongest appetite of the moment. He is aware of himself and his appetites and comes to learn what objects they seek. He can reflect upon his experience, grasp as a whole the situation in which he finds himself, and, what is most important, objectify his own feelings and desires, so as to pass judgment upon them in the light of that situation. So he is able to appreciate the circumstances in which desires conflict and to seek means of resolving conflicts and of attaining a satisfaction not just of particular appetites but of himself as a person. This capacity is what entitles man to the epithet "rational." Having a modicum of rationality, men in a situation of conflict restrain and order their desires so as to gain greater satisfaction on the whole, on the one hand by disciplining themselves so as to bring their natural impulses into harmony, and on the other by co-operating socially in the effort to supply their common needs. Such co-operation itself demands regulation and organization of conduct involving self-restraint and discipline. The ordering of conduct, both for internal harmony of the individual personality and for social co-ordination (strictly only two aspects of one and the same process), often gives rise to a tension between what one desires at any particular moment and what is desirable on the whole, in one's own interest and in the interests of others on whom one is dependent and with whom one's own interest is inescapably and inseparately associated. It results in the antithesis of inclination and duty and imposes upon each of us obligations to do what is in the ultimate interest of all. The outcome is an organized pattern of social life, found through long experience—indeed, the experience of many generations—to be the most satisfactory on the whole. It is a way of life which entails elaborate regulation of conduct, and therefore obligation to act against one's own inclination whenever that conflicts with the requirements of the total pattern.

This is the answer to the first part of our first question but it remains to say why we have an obligation to respect persons as such. It is easy to see why we should have a duty to respect the members of our own society, for the interest of all though common, is made up of and exists only through the interest of each. Social good and individual good are mutually dependent. Without the second the first cannot exist. The realization of a common good is at the same time the realization of a personal good, both because the latter is impossible without the former (for we are essentially social beings and can satisfy none of our needs adequately without mutual help) and because the former is meaningless without the latter. What nobody enjoys individually cannot be enjoyed in common. The ultimate aim of the whole social way of life is the fullest possible development of the capacities of the individuals who make up the society concerned, giving the fullest possible satisfaction of the complete personality.

This complete development and satisfaction of the individual as an integrated personality is the ultimate criterion of all human value. Whatever has value for human beings does so only if and so far as it contributes to the full realization of personality, whether it be material wealth, intellectual cultivation, art, scientific discovery, or moral integrity. Some of these are subordinate to others in the final assessment; for the realization of personal capacities is by no means restricted (as we are sometimes apt to think) to the development of intellectual and artistic accomplishments. The condition of that is the existence and maintenance of harmonious and fruitful relations between co-operating persons in a social order which requires each to subordinate his own immediate advantage to the general interest (or more properly, to identify his own ultimate welfare with the common good). The realization of moral capacities is therefore fundamental to the development of personality generally and in any possible conflict of values must take precedence. In sum, the full and satisfactory realization of human personality is attainable only in a complete way of life, led with knowledge and insight into the principles, moral, philosophical and religious, which govern its satisfactory character. It was this, or something like it, that Aristotle had in mind when he defined the good for man as "an activity of the soul in accordance with excellence, in a complete life."

It is obvious that this "end for man" can be realized only in persons, and it follows that each and every person is himself of ultimate worth as the final source and vehicle of value. The moral end is human welfare, and moral obligation is the obligation so to act as to achieve the greatest possible human welfare that the circumstances permit. Just how, in detail, human welfare is to be attained is not the subject of this paper, but we now have at least an indication as to how the first of our three main questions may be answered. The ground of our obligation to respect persons as such (at least in our own society) is that each and every person is of intrinsic worth as the ultimate source and vehicle of all the values that society aims at realizing. For this reason every person is an end in himself and may not be treated as a mere means (or as a mere obstacle) to the satisfaction of others.

Against this position it might be argued that if it were accepted the conclusion would not follow, for if the realization of personal capacity is the goal of all endeavor, then in any situation such that fuller realization for some persons was attainable only by using others as a mere means (by enslaving them or liquidating them altogether), so long as on balance more value was ultimately realized, it would be right to sacrifice the interests of the minority to that of the majority. This objection seems to me to make two unwarrantable assumptions. First, it assumes that the fulfillment of human personality, which as I have said essentially involves the realization of moral capacity, *could be* better achieved by sacrificing the welfare of some to that of others; and secondly, it assumes that value is something like ice cream, of which there is a limited quantity so that if some people are deprived of it altogether others will enjoy more. But neither is the case.

The first assumption is that the perfection of human character is largely a matter of creating favorable circumstances, easier living conditions, and removing problems. This widely held view is fallacious. True it is that social organization and much of our activity aims at these things; and we have today succeeded in developing the most complex and elaborate techniques for better living and for problem-solving. But the more we progress in this way, the more difficult it becomes to maintain the standards we have set ourselves in scientific achievement, economic organization and political procedure. If we fail to meet the demands set by these standards our civilization will crumble and our personal achievements decline. It is only by meeting the difficulties not by obliterating them that we can progress further. In support of this point let me quote Ortega y Gasset:

There might be a deceptive tendency to believe that a life born into a world of plenty should be better, more really a life than one which consists in a struggle against scarcity. Such is not the case. . . .[2]

Quite the contrary. A world superabundant in possibilities automatically produces deformities, vicious types of human life. . . . the average man take [s] his place in a world of superabundance, of which he perceives only the lavishness of the means at his disposal, nothing of the pains involved. He finds himself surrounded by marvelous comfortable privileges. On the other hand he is ignorant how difficult it is to invent those machines and those instruments and to assure their production in the future; he does not realize how unstable is the organization of the State and is scarcely conscious to himself of any obligations. This lack of balance falsifies his nature, vitiates it in its very roots, causing him to lose contact with the very substance of life, which is made up of absolute danger, is radically problematic.[3]

The sacrifice of some persons in a community for the sake of a presumed greater self-realization on the part of the rest would only be presumed efficacious if the removal of the minority eased the problems which the remainder would have to face. But if Ortega is right (and I believe he is) it would follow that even if the assumption were true, a decline instead of an improvement in the level of human personal development would result.

To believe otherwise would also be to misconceive the nature of value in the way already mentioned. Not only is it the case that many of the higher values are constituted in large measure by the difficulty of achievement, but also the more important forms of value—and perhaps, in the last analysis, all values—are not of the competitive sort, such that they can be attained by some persons only if others are deprived of them. The most important values can be enjoyed by any persons only if and to the extent that they are enjoyed by all.

2 *The Revolt of the Masses* (New York, 1957), p. 98.
3 *Ibid.*, pp. 100–2.

They are more like the pleasure of playing in a symphony than that of eating ice cream. It is only so far as every member of the orchestra plays at his best that the symphony can be fully enjoyed, and unless the musicians were very unskilled, it would be nonsense to suggest that by eliminating a portion of the score and silencing a proportion of the instruments a more satisfactory result could be achieved by the remainder. One does not normally improve the quality of performance by shooting a number of the players. The pursuit of human welfare, likewise, is a joint endeavor which can only be attained by common effort, though it can only be realized in individual persons. Consequently, every person is of importance to every other as a partner in the enterprise, and the loss or sacrifice of any, is a loss, in some degree at least, for all. If some individuals assume the opposite, they fail by that very fact, and by any conduct based upon that assumption, to realize in themselves the moral values which are essential to their own personal fulfillment, just as the musician (as Plato pointed out in the *Republic*[4]) who attempts to overreach his colleagues ruins the performance, both for them and for himself.

Being treated as an end is not, however, incompatible with serving at the same time and in some measure as a means to others' satisfaction—for in a society where people help and serve one another they are all mutually means and ends. We may say that a person may not be *treated* by others as a mere means, but that he can serve as a means to the welfare of others so long as he identifies his own interest with theirs and realizes himself in his service of them. He is then at once both means and end.

(2) I now have to explain why this duty which we owe to the members of our own society should be extended to all persons without distinction, whether they belong to our own group or any others. This will include the answer to the second question. To some extent we have answered it already,

[4] *Republic* I, 349e.

for if we recognize that personality is the ultimate vehicle and criterion of value, it should follow that this is true of persons in any society, and obligations of members of one group to those of another will arise out of the mutual relations of groups, just as obligations of each individual to others in his own group arise out of their mutual social relationships. But something further can be said in support of the view that human beings as such have an intrinsic worth of which their social nature is a sign and a consequence as much as a source.

It was remarked earlier that men control their passions and desires and organize their activities in society because they have "a modicum of rationality," a capacity to see things together, to recognize conflicts and inconsistencies in their own and in others' conduct, and to discern the means of resolving them and of pursuing their own best satisfaction. This capacity for self-objectification is part and parcel of the ability to think systematically: that is, to see things in relation and the relevance of one thing to another. It is thus, at the same time, the capacity to think referentially, to symbolize and to evaluate. It makes speech possible and likewise art—all such activities as depend upon the use and recognition of symbolic form. Because it enables a man to objectify his appetites and feelings, to compare them and the objects of their satisfaction, it enables him to weigh their importance as contributing to his ultimate satisfaction. It is the capacity for conceiving himself, as a self, as a person, distinguishable from and superior to passing and ephemeral desires and pleasures, and for seeking a more complete and permanent fulfillment. Consequently, it is rationality—not simply as a skill or accomplishment in the use of instrumental intellectual techniques—but rationality as described above: as the power of self-objectification and self-organization, which does not simply abstract from feeling but which informs, refines and resolves the conflicts within feeling, which transforms man from a mere appetitive animal to a person. It is at once the ability to evaluate, the source of value and its criterion. It is the instrument of realization, while at the same time its perfection is the aim of all endeavor. As embodied in persons it thus becomes the one object of intrinsic worth that demands universal respect. It is this that is meant by the dictum of religion that man is created in the image of God. Consequently, the respect due to persons is not limited to any social group or to any set of special circumstances, but only to their identification as what for short we may conveniently call rational beings. This leads us to the third main question that we raised: How do we define and identify persons?

IV. WHAT IS A PERSON?

(3) The definition is already by implication at hand: A person is a self-conscious, self-objectifying, rational being, in a sense of rational which sees "reason" as a constructive, organizing principle of thought, not simply as an abstracting instrument of analysis in the service of the passions (as Hume alleged). Though here it is not possible to enter into detailed discussion of this antithesis, it may be mentioned in explanation that feeling and appetite are not devoid of structural activity but manifest the same constructive principle at a lower level of realization as does reason at a more developed stage of consciousness. The latter is a development out of the former in complicated ways (which cannot now be explicated). Appetition and feeling are organic activities tending towards a form of completeness which only becomes fully explicit in self-conscious endeavor. Thus reason is not "the slave of the passions" but their leader and guide for which they provide the energy and drive. How, then, can we apply this definition so as to identify persons as the universal object of respect?

The answer may seem palpably simple. Anybody with the least potentiality of human rational and moral development, or to whom such potentiality can be imputed, qualifies as a person. As such his right to consideration and to treatment as an end in himself must be respected for his intrinsic worth as an ultimate source and vehicle of value.

This conclusion is in some measure supported by the legal definition of persons as the subjects of rights and duties. They must be alive and they must be human, but this is not what, for the law, defines their personality. What does that is simply the inherence in them of rights and duties.[5] Before the law even infants *in utero* may have rights. Responsibility is not an indispensable condition: the insane also have legal rights and so are legal persons; and to say this is no more than to say that other persons have duties towards them— that they are worthy of respect. But the legal definition (as is so often the case with the law) is circular, because to be the subject of a right is the same as to be entitled to respect, and if that defines legal personality, all we are told by the definition is that a person is anybody entitled to respect; and then to rule that all persons are so entitled is purely analytic.

Moreover, that every human being should rank in this way as a person is not as obvious as it may seem at first sight, because some human individuals appear incapable of intellectual or moral development and so of the realization of value. Should such people be respected at the expense of others who have definite potentialities? Are such people to be regarded as persons? Aristotle was prepared to justify slavery on the ground that some men were incapable of conducting their own affairs and so were fit only to be living instruments. They were, he said, "slaves by nature." This involved him in the implicit admission that some men were not rational and so were incapable of happiness as he defined it. But if so (according to his view) they were not men. This may be the proper conclusion to draw from his argument: that as all men are by nature rational, all are capable of self-direction and, therefore, none are slaves by nature.

But should we not limit the title to rational personality to those who are responsible for their actions? What are we to

[5] Cf. Sir T. E. Holland, *Elements of Jurisprudence* (Oxford, 1924), p. 96.

say of individuals who are moronic or insane or simply immature? Are infants, imbeciles and madmen also to be respected as rational persons? Might we not exclude them from the classification, or if we admit them as persons, could we not make them exceptions from the principle of respect? If we were to concur, our only justifiable pretext for taking either course would be that such persons were altogether incapable of responsible action.

Common sentiment, however, would not support any such restriction, for we normally do acknowledge duties towards people who are not regarded as responsible, and this implies that they are persons worthy of "respect" in our special sense of the word. We commonly consider that parents, teachers and others have obligations towards children, in fact the latter's very immaturity increases our sense of obligation. We commonly acknowledge duties to care for, protect and give asylum to the mentally deranged and deficient. Lack of responsibility on their part does not absolve others, we usually think, from responsibility towards them. Are we then wrong to recognize such obligations? Clearly infants and the merely immature should present no problem, because they qualify as persons with intrinsic value on account of their potentiality for development as responsible agents. But the hopelessly and incurably cretinous or insane may give us pause. In what way are they "rational," in what degree are they sources and vehicles of ultimate value? What potentiality have they for the realization of human capacities? It would seem, virtually none.

Here, we can narrow the field still further, because with respect to the insane generally we may well be in a similar position to Aristotle's with respect to slaves. His doctrine collapses as soon as we try to make precise (as he did not) what degree of capacity is needed to direct one's own affairs. The view that the insane are totally incapable of responsible action may similarly collapse when we try to make precise the notion of insanity. This, as Dr. Szasz emphasizes in another paper of this volume, we are far from being able to do, in spite of our growing medical and psychiatric knowledge. Progress in these fields, on the contrary, seems to support the view that no clear distinction can be drawn between the mentally ill and the mentally normal. To treat the former as if they were not persons with the same sort of rights as the latter would not therefore be justified. We cannot regard them simply as obstacles to the satisfactions and convenience of others, and whatever measures we take in dealing with their behavioral aberrations, we ought always to take them with *their* welfare in mind as well as that of other people. Moreover, however difficult and extreme the case of insanity, and however apparently incurable, we can at least always hope for improvement. We cannot know for sure that the patient's internal make-up will not become so modified as to rectify his outward behavior, or that no new remedial techniques will be discovered to which he would respond. He remains, therefore, a potential medium for the realization of value and retains the right to be treated as an end in himself.

The most difficult case is that of the extreme mentally deficient, for here the potentiality for development seems to be at a minimum. But, here again, we cannot *a priori* rule out the possibility that some development might occur, either through new discoveries during the lifetime of the moron, or through some physiological change which medical prognosis failed to anticipate. If both these eventualities should seem too improbable, it would still be wrong to sacrifice a mentally defective person for the sake of others more fortunate. To do so would, in the first place, be an act of callousness the implications of which, for our general way of life would be most deleterious. If we can treat persons with one sort of deficiency as expendable, why not those with other sorts of incapacity? If it were considered right to treat persons who were apparently incurably deficient as expendable it would become habitual, and that propensity to active sympathy of which Maclagan speaks would be so far undermined and would tend to become attentuated in other cases also where the justification would be even more doubtful. Again, what degree of mental incapacity is to disqualify a person from sympathetic consideration? and who is qualified to be the judge? Who is able to decide precisely what the experience of such persons may be, and to judge that it is entirely worthless? Whoever undertook to disqualify them as persons would have to assume a responsibility for which little short of omniscience would be the condition.

Nevertheless, objections may be raised to what I have maintained on the ground of injustice. Surely, you may say, it is not right to sacrifice the welfare of persons, who are clearly capable of realizing perhaps the highest values, for the sake of hopeless cretins or criminal lunatics or others of that sort. Is it just to devote the resources of society to the preservation of such people, to condemn the mentally healthy to spend time and energy caring for them and to risk being harmed by their unpredictably dangerous behavior?

The answer clearly cannot be a simple one. Obviously it is wrong to sacrifice normal people to the interests of abnormal, but by the same token it would be wrong to do the converse. And the consideration and treatment to which any person is entitled should be commensurate with his potentiality. What that is may be roughly gauged for practical purposes, but, for a number of reasons, cannot be precisely assessed. Where a choice has to be made between the interests of someone who has obvious potentiality and someone who has obviously very little, the apportionment of opportunities should favor the former. But we never have a right to treat either as entirely negligible. Furthermore, it must never be forgotten that among the capacities and values to be realized, the most important are moral potentialities and values, and these include the virtues of compassion and devotion to the welfare of others. Consequently, those who devote themselves to the care of the incapacitated may by so doing be realizing in themselves greater values than they would if they applied their talents to more selfish pursuits. If we regard their welfare as comprising no more than their own convenience, we are failing to respect *them* as persons and are insulting them by overlooking *their* moral capacity.[6]

Again, to neglect the claims of the apparently incapable on account of their incapacity is a sort of defeatism, for it abandons the opportunity to study and investigate difficult cases and so the means of ever discovering how they might come to be remedied. We can, for instance, only discover ways of ameliorating, curing and preventing cretinism and insanity by caring for and studying the insane, not just as scientific specimens, but as potential persons.

We may thus confirm the answer to the second question with which we began, that every human being, however immature or defective, who has any mental capacity at all, is a person and is worthy of respect.

V. APPLICATIONS

The principle of respect for persons is fundamental in morals and is the key to many moral problems and political issues. It would be interesting to pursue its ramifications systematically, but I have time only to select a few examples at random.

(i) The principle of respect applies to our treatment of criminals as well as of lunatics but with somewhat different and complementary implications. In considering the importance of responsibility as a criterion of personality I argued that it was not indispensable, but this was only if and when we have some reason to believe the individual potentially responsible or hope that he may become so. It should be obvious that responsibility is an essential attribute of personality. On the one hand, our concern for the mentally disturbed is largely lest they be treated too easily as irresponsible when their behavior may, in fact, be only socially eccentric and aberrant. On the other hand, our treatment of criminals may,

[6] This is not an argument for the value as persons of the patients, but against the allegation of injustice to their guardians.

with the best of intentions, show insufficient respect if we treat them too readily as patients. No doubt much criminal behavior may be due to bad social conditions and to psychological causes amenable to treatment, but if we assume that the subject has no moral capacity at all, and treat crime as no different from disease, are we not failing to show proper respect for the personality of the criminal, who may even claim as a right moral as well as psychological correction? He is liable to resent pathology more than punishment, and to find it, as in some sense it is, insulting to his *amour propre*.

Yet, to carry retribution to excessive lengths may be no less violation of the same moral principle. The question of capital punishment is largely a question of the expendability or justifiable destructibility of those whose moral decrepitude is extreme. This is not simply a question of justice. The brutal and wanton murderer may deserve to die, but who has a right to destroy him and on what moral ground? If incurable idiocy is no justification for the liquidation of the affected persons, is moral incorrigibility any better justification? First, we must observe that the great majority of murderers, even the most depraved, are not obviously incorrigible morally, and secondly, that even when a criminal seems hopelessly and irremediably immoral, we have no guarantee that his merely human judges are infallible. Here again it is a presumption of omniscience to decide that any person is morally worthless, to the extent that we can justifiably put him to death. If the death sentence can ever rightly be pronounced it can only be by God.

(ii) Another way in which we are apt to fail in our respect for persons is by intolerance of their political opinions or their religious beliefs. More fundamental than a man's responsibility for overt action is his responsibility for judgment, belief, and opinion. These we hold, if we hold them genuinely, because we have formed them ourselves by whatever logical or psychological process. There is no other genuine way of holding an opinion or subscribing to a belief. The attempt to force other people to adopt beliefs and opinions (whether

religious or political) which we think right is thus a deroga-
tion of their personal integrity—a failure of respect, because it
presumes that their own capacity to form opinions is not
merely deficient but wholly lacking. Such treatment is a de-
traction from their rationality. To present them with arguments on the assumption that they are reasonable beings
capable of judgment on the basis of evidence is to respect
their personalities, but to attempt to force or cajole them into
accepting a point of view just because we ourselves think it
is true, even though we believe it to be for their own good, is
to treat them as if they were not rational and responsible
persons. And to ostracize them or discriminate socially against
them merely on account of their beliefs would be altogether
unjustified.

(iii) In these examples the issues are subtle and difficult to
decide, but we are all familiar today with others the rights
and wrongs of which are more blatant. Racial discrimination,
in all its forms, involves violation of the principle of respect,
for it discriminates on grounds irrelevant to personality. Social
differences of one sort or another are unavoidable in every
society but they are just (as Plato demonstrated) only if
they are based on personal capacity and merit. To discriminate on any other ground is unjust. It is only persons, recognized as such, who have rights so that respect for persons is
implied in justice. But justice is not the same as respect for
persons even if it presupposes such respect. Racial discrimination, however, as we witness it today in many places, goes far
beyond mere injustice. There are people in this country, in
South Africa and elsewhere, who discriminate in their personal and also in their official relations between white persons
and colored, in a way which implies that colored people are
not really persons at all. The color of the skin is taken as the
only relevant qualification for personality and the non-white
is treated as non-human. The enormity of this attitude, if it
is not immediately apparent, becomes so if we substitute some
other accidental characteristic for skin-color: for instance, the
color of the hair or eyes, or the weight or height of the indi-

vidual. Racial characteristics are really not more pertinent than these. What we witness today, however, is not only racial discrimination but deliberate maltreatment of Negroes for no reason other than their color. To assault or murder anybody is a criminal act; for the police to deprive persons of the protection of the law is injustice and is itself a crime. But in many places today we find white men who treat their white associates with proper consideration, going to considerable lengths to behave criminally towards Negroes, and white officials, who carry out their functions scrupulously with respect to white citizens, deliberately victimizing non-whites. Such behavior is not just ordinarily criminal or immoral, it is a special effort on the part of the agent to demonstrate his refusal to recognize moral obligation towards persons of color. In other words it is a deliberate refusal to recognize their rights as persons for no reason other than the color of their skins.

But to act thus is, in principle, precisely the same as to practice slavery. It is equally the refusal to respect persons and to treat some as if they were unworthy of proper consideration and as if we had no moral obligation towards them. The precise opposite of this is St. Paul's exhortation to Philemon, revealing a spirit morally far superior to our attitudes at the present day. He sends back Onesimus "no longer as a slave but as a dear brother." He cuts away the whole basis of slavery, replacing it by its moral antithesis: active concern for the person as a person. Such concern is incompatible with slavery because the person so treated is not (and cannot be) used as a mere instrument. Consequently, our modern society still has some way to go if it is to claim moral superiority to the civilizations of antiquity. Abolition of the institution of slavery is not enough; what is still lacking is the abandonment of the spirit of slavery and the unqualified adoption of the principle of respect for persons.

ETHICS AND REVOLUTION

Herbert Marcuse

HERBERT MARCUSE is Professor of Philosophy at the University of California, San Diego. He has taught at Brandeis, Columbia, and Harvard Universities and at the Institute of Social Research in New York. He has worked at the Office of Strategic Services and the Office of Intelligence Research in the United States State Department. He has published extensively in English and in German, and his books include *Reason and Revolution* (1941), *Eros and Civilization* (1955), *Soviet Marxism* (1958), and *One Dimensional Man* (1964).

I propose to discuss the relation between ethics and revolution by taking as guidance the following question: Can a revolution be justified as right, as good, perhaps even as necessary, and justified not merely in political terms (as expedient for certain interests) but in ethical terms, that is to say, justified with respect to the human condition as such, to the potential of man in a given historical situation? This means that ethical terms such as "right" or "good" will be applied to political and social movements, with the hypothesis that the moral evaluation of such movements is (in a sense to be defined) more than subjective, more than a matter of preference. Under this hypothesis, "good" and "right" would mean serving to establish, to promote, or to extend human freedom and happiness in a commonwealth, regardless of the form of government. This preliminary definition combines individual and personal, private and public welfare. It tries to recapture a basic concept of classical political philosophy which has been all too often repressed, namely, that the end of government is not only the greatest possible freedom, but also the greatest possible happiness of man, that is to say, a life without fear and misery, and a life in peace.

Here we encounter the first vexing question, namely, who determines, who can and by what right determine the general interest of a commonwealth, and thereby determine the range and limits of individual freedom and happiness, and the sacrifices imposed upon individual freedom and happiness in the name and on behalf of the commonwealth? For as long as the general and individual welfare do not immediately coincide, the latter will be *made* to conform with the former. And if we ask this question we are at once confronted with an equally serious and embarrassing problem: granted even that freedom is not only an individual and private affair, that it is rather determined by the society, by the state in which we live, what about happiness? Is the happiness of an individual his own private affair, or is it too, in a very definite sense, subject to the limitations and even the definitions imposed upon it by a commonwealth? The extreme position that human happiness is and must remain individual and the individual's own affair cannot be defended if we give it only a few minutes' thought. There are certainly modes and types of individual happiness which cannot be tolerated by any kind of commonwealth. It is perfectly possible—as a matter of fact we know it to be the fact—that the people who were the master torturers in the Hitler concentration camps were often quite happy doing their job. This is one of the many cases of individual happiness where we do not hesitate to say that it is not merely the individual himself who can be and who can remain the judge of his own happiness. We assume a tribunal which is (actually or morally) entitled to "define" individual happiness.

Now after these preliminary clarifications, let me define what I mean by "revolution." By "revolution" I understand the overthrow of a legally established government and constitution by a social class or movement with the aim of altering the social as well as the political structure. This definition excludes all military coups, palace revolutions, and "preventive" counterrevolutions (such as Fascism and Nazism) because they do not alter the basic social structure. If we define revolution in this way we can move one step forward by saying that such a radical and qualitative change implies violence. Peaceful revolutions, if there are such things, if there can be such things, do not present any problem. We can therefore reformulate the initial question by asking: Is the revolutionary use of violence justifiable as a means for establishing or promoting human freedom and happiness? The question implies a very important assumption, namely, that there are rational criteria for determining the possibilities of human freedom and happiness available to a society in a specific historical situation. If there are no such rational criteria, it would be impossible to evaluate a political movement in terms of its chances to attain a greater extent or a higher degree of freedom and happiness in society.

But postulating the availability of rational standards and criteria for judging the given possibilities of human freedom and happiness means assuming that the ethical, moral standards are *historical* standards. If they are not, they remain meaningless abstractions. Applied to our question, this means that to claim an ethical and moral right, a revolutionary movement must be able to give rational grounds for its chances to grasp real possibilities of human freedom and happiness, and it must be able to demonstrate the adequacy of its means for obtaining this end. Only if the problem is placed in such a historical context, is it susceptible to rational discussion. Otherwise, only two positions remain open, namely, to reject *a priori* or to endorse *a priori* all revolution and revolutionary violence. Both positions, the affirmative as well as the negative one, offend against historical facts. It is, for example, meaningless to say that modern society *could* have come about without the English, American, and French Revolutions. It is also meaningless to say that all revolutionary violence had the same social function and consequences. The violence of the Civil Wars in seventeenth century England, the violence of the first French Revolution certainly had effects and consequences very different from those of the Bolshevik Revolution, and very different from the counterrevolutionary violence perpetrated by the Nazi and Fascist regimes. Moreover, the positions of *a priori* rejecting or *a priori* approving social and political violence would amount to sanctioning any change brought about in history, regardless of whether it would be in a progressive or regressive, liberating or enslaving direction.

A very brief glance at the historical development of our problem may facilitate the discussion. In classical political philosophy, revolutions were not considered as breaks of the historical continuum. Plato as well as Aristotle believed that revolutions were built into the very dynamic of politics, that they belonged to the historical and at the same time natural cycle of birth, growth and decay of political forms. In medieval and early modern philosophy the idea of a natural and divine order either outlawed all resistance to established government, or made resistance against tyranny not only a right but a moral duty and obligation. Then, in the sixteenth and seventeenth centuries, the practically unlimited right to resist a government, even to overthrow a government, was normally claimed by Protestant against Catholic, and by Catholic against Protestant regimes. A most characteristic reaction against these doctrines may be seen in the attitude towards revolution which we find in such different figures as Hobbes and Descartes, namely, that change is always to the worst. Leave the established social and political institutions as they are, for, no matter how bad they may be, the risk of overthrowing them is too great. Descartes, the great revolutionary in thought, was extremely conservative with respect to the "great public bodies." To them, doubt is not supposed to be extended, they are supposed to be left alone. At the same time, philosophers are strongly inclined to endorse a revolution once it has proved to be successful. Representative of this attitude is the case of Kant—certainly not a paragon of opportunism and expediency—who rejected the right of resistance and condemned revolt against established government, but added that, once a revolution has succeeded, a new legal government is established, and man owes obedience to the new revolutionary government just as he owed it to the government which was overthrown by the revolution.

On the other side of the fence, political theory and practice recognize historical situations in which violence becomes the necessary and essential element of progress. This concept is instrumental in the political theory and practice of totalitarian democracy. Robespierre calls for the "despotism of liberty" against the despotism of tyranny: in the fight for freedom, in the interest of the whole against the particular interests of oppression, terror may become a necessity and an obligation. Here, violence, revolutionary violence, appears not only as a political means but as a moral duty. The terror is defined as *counter*violence: it is "legitimate" only in defense against the oppressors and until they are defeated. Similarly, the Marxian concept of proletarian dictatorship is that of a transitional self-cancelling dictatorship: self-cancelling because it is supposed to last only as long as the power of the old ruling classes still combats the construction of the socialist society; after their defeat, the engines of repression were to be stopped. Here too, revolutionary violence is defined as counterviolence. The Marxian concept assumes that the old ruling classes would never voluntarily abdicate their position, that they would be the first to use violence against the revolution, and that revolutionary violence would be the defense against counterrevolutionary violence.

The theory of an educational, transitional dictatorship implies the paradoxical proposition that man must be "forced to be free." Political philosophy has always recognized the moral function of coercion (the coercive power of law, either above the sovereign or identical with the sovereign), but Rousseau provides a radically new justification. Coercion is necessitated by the immoral, repressive conditions under which men live. The basic idea is: how can slaves who do not even know they are slaves free themselves? How can they liberate themselves by their own power, by their own faculties? How can they spontaneously accomplish liberation? They must be taught and must be led to be free, and this the more so the more the society in which they live uses all available means in order to shape and preform their consciousness and to make it immune against possible alternatives. This idea of an educational, preparatory dictatorship has today become an integral element of revolution and of the justification of the revolutionary oppression. The dictatorships which began as revolutionary dictatorships and then perpetuated themselves claim to be in their very essence and structure transitional and preparatory for a stage at which they can be abolished by virtue of their own achievements.

The main argument against the notion of the transitional dictatorship is usually condensed in the question: who educates the educators? By what right do those who actually exercise the dictatorship speak in the name of freedom and happiness as general conditions? This argument by itself is not sufficient, because in a lesser degree it applies even to non-authoritarian societies, where the policy-making top layer is not constantly and effectively controlled from below. However, even if we concede that the majority of men are not yet free today, and that their liberation cannot be spontaneous, the question still remains whether the dictatorial means are adequate to attain the end, namely, liberation. In other words the question of a transitional dictatorship cannot be separated from the general question of whether there can be such a thing as a moral justification of suppression and violence in a revolution. I shall now briefly discuss this question.

The historical revolutions were usually advocated and started in the name of freedom, or rather in the name of greater freedom for more strata of the population. We must first examine this claim strictly on empirical grounds. Human freedom is not and never has been a static condition but an historical condition, a process which involves the radical alteration, and even negation, of established ways of life. The form and content of freedom change with every new stage in the development of civilization, which is man's increasing mastery of man and nature. In both modes, mastery means domination, control; more effective control of nature makes for more effective control of man. Obviously, the possibilities of human freedom and happiness in advanced industrial society today are in no way comparable with those available, even theoretically available, at preceding stages of history. Thus, with respect to the form, extent, degree and content of human freedom, we deal with strictly historical and changing conditions. We can say even more. Measured against the real possibilities of freedom, we always live in a state of relative unfreedom. The wide gap between real possibility and actuality, between the rational and the real has never been closed. Freedom always presupposes liberation, or a step from one state of freedom and unfreedom to a subsequent state. With the advance of technical progress, the later state is *potentially* (but by no means actually!) a *higher* stage, that is, quantitatively and qualitatively. But if this is the case, if freedom always presupposes liberation from unfree and unhappy conditions, it means that this liberation always offends against and ultimately subverts established and sanctioned institutions and interests. In history, they never abdicated voluntarily. Consequently, if and when freedom is a process of liberation, a transition from lower, more restricted forms of freedom to higher forms of freedom, then it always, no matter how, offends against the existing and established state of affairs. And precisely on this ground revolutionary violence has been most effectively justified as counterviolence, that is, as violence necessary in order to secure higher forms of freedom against the resistance of the established forms.

The ethics of revolution thus testifies to the clash and conflict of two historical rights: on the one side, the right of that which *is*, the established commonwealth on which the life and perhaps even the happiness of the individuals depend; and on the other side, the right of that which *can* be and perhaps even *ought* to be because it may reduce toil, misery, and injustice, provided always that this chance can be demonstrated as a real possibility. Such a demonstration must provide rational criteria; we can now add: these must be *historical* criteria. As such, they amount to an "historical calculus," namely, calculation of the chances of a future society as against the chances of the existing society with respect to human progress, that is to say, technical and material progress used in such a way that it increases individual freedom and happiness. Now if such an historical calculus is to have any rational basis, it must, on the one side, take into account the sacrifices exacted from the living generations on behalf of the established society, the established law and order, the number of victims made in defense of this society in war and peace, in the struggle for existence, individual and national. The calculus would further have to take into account the intellectual and material resources available to the society and the manner in which they are actually used with respect to their full capacity of satisfying vital human needs and pacifying the struggle for existence. On the other side, the historical calculus would have to project the chances of the contesting revolutionary movement of improving the prevailing conditions, namely, whether the revolutionary plan or program demonstrates the technical, material, and mental possibility of reducing the sacrifices and the number of victims. Even prior to the question as to the possibility of such a calculus (which, I believe, does exist), its inhuman quantifying character is evident. But its inhumanity is that of history itself, token of its empirical, rational foundation. No hypocrisy should from the beginning distort the examination. Nor is this brutal calculus an empty intellectual abstraction; in fact, at its decisive turns, history became such a calculated experiment.

The ethics of revolution, if there is such a thing, will therefore be in accordance not with absolute, but with historical standards. They do not cancel the validity of those general norms which formulate requirements for the progress of mankind toward humanity. No matter how rationally one may justify revolutionary means in terms of the demonstrable chance of obtaining freedom and happiness for future generations, and thereby justify violating existing rights and liberties and life itself, there are forms of violence and suppression which no revolutionary situation can justify because they negate the very end for which the revolution is a means. Such are arbitrary violence, cruelty, and indiscriminate terror. However, within the historical continuum, revolutions establish a moral and ethical code of their own and in this way become the origin, the fountainhead and source of new general norms and values. In fact some of today's most generally-professed values originated in revolutions, for example, the value of tolerance in the English Civil Wars, the inalienable rights of man in the American and French Revolutions. These ideas become an historical force, first as partial ideas, instruments of a revolutionary movement for specific political ends. Their realization originally involved violence; they then assumed not only partial political but general ethical validity and rejected violence. In this way, revolutions place themselves under ethical standards.

Violence *per se* has never been made a revolutionary value by the leaders of the historical revolutions. His contemporaries rejected Georges Sorel's attempt to cut the link between violence and reason, which was at the same time the attempt to free the class struggle from all ethical considerations. In comparing the violence of the class struggle in its revolutionary phase with the violence of military operations in war, he made the former subject to strategic calculations only: the end was the total defeat of the enemy; violence a means to attain this end—the relation between means and end was a technical one. Sorel's defense of violence this side of good and evil remained isolated from the revolutionary reality of his time; if he had any influence, it was on the side of the counterrevolution. Otherwise, violence was defended, not *per se*, but as part of rational suppression, suppression of counterrevolutionary activity, of established rights and privileges, and, for the society at large, of material and intellectual needs, that is, enforcement of austerity, rationing, censorship. Now this suppression which includes violence is practiced in the interest of the objectives of the revolution, and these objectives are presented not only as political but also as moral values, ethical imperatives, namely greater freedom for the greater number of people. And in this sense the objectives and the ends of the revolution itself claim general validity and become subject to moral standards and evaluation.

Here we are confronted with the problem of all ethics, namely, the question as to the ultimate sanction of moral values. Or, in plain language, who or what determines the validity of ethical norms? The question becomes acute only with the secularization of the West; it was no problem in the Middle Ages as long as a transcendent sanction of ethics was accepted. The infidels could justly be exterminated, heretics could justly be burned—in spite of all protest. This was justice in terms of the prevailing values, which in turn were those of transcendent ethics. But today, where is the sanction of ethical values—sanction not in terms of the enforcement but in terms of the acceptance of ethical values, the proof of their validity? Sanction today, it seems, rests mainly in a precarious and flexible syndrome of custom, fear, utility, and religion; flexible because, within the syndrome, there is a large range of change. I refer, for example, to the high degree of liberalization in sexual morality which we have witnessed during the last thirty years, or, to the easy suspension of practically all ethical values in so-called emergency situations. The sanction and validity of ethical norms is thus restricted to the normal state of affairs in social and political relations.

Now in terms of the normal established state of affairs, a revolution is by definition immoral; it offends against the right of the existing commonwealth; it permits and even demands deception, cunning, suppression, destruction of life and property, and so on. But a judgment by definition is an inadequate judgment. Ethical standards by virtue of their imperative claim transcend any given state of affairs, and they transcend it, not to any metaphysical entities but to the historical continuum in which every given state of affairs has emerged, by which every given state of affairs is defined, and in which every given state of affairs will be altered and surpassed by other states. And in the historical continuum which defines its place and function, the ethics of revolution appeal to an historical calculus. Can the intended new society, the society intended by the revolution, offer better chances for progress in freedom than the existing society? In the historical continuum, these chances can only be measured by going beyond the given state of affairs, going beyond it not simply into an abstract vacuum of speculation, but going beyond it by calculating the resources, intellectual as well as material, scientific as well as technical, available to a given society, and projecting the most rational ways of utilizing these resources. Now if such projection is possible, then it can yield objective criteria for judging revolutions as to their historical function in terms of progress or regression, in terms of the development of *humanitas*.

A preliminary answer is suggested by a glance at the historical process itself. Historically, the objective tendency of the great revolutions of the modern period was the enlargement of the social range of freedom and the enlargement of the satisfaction of needs. No matter how much the social interpretations of the English and French Revolutions may differ, they seem to agree in that a redistribution of the social wealth took place, so that previously less privileged or underprivileged classes were the beneficiaries of this change, economically and/or politically. In spite of subsequent periods of reaction and restoration, the result and objective function of these revolutions was the establishment of more liberal governments, a gradual democratization of society, and technical progress. I said "objective function" because this evaluation of the revolution is obviously a judgment *ex post facto*. The intention and ideology of the leaders of the revolution, and the drives of the masses may have had quite different aims and motives. By virtue of their objective function, these revolutions attained progress in the sense defined, namely, a demonstrable enlargement of the range of human freedom; they thus established, in spite of the terrible sacrifices exacted by them, an ethical right over and above all political justification.

But if such ethical right and its criteria are always and necessarily after the fact, it serves for nought and leaves us with the irrational choice of either *a priori* accepting or *a priori* rejecting all revolution. Now I submit that, while the historical function of a revolution becomes identifiable only after the fact, its prospective direction, progressive or regressive is, with the certainty of a reasonable *chance*, demonstrable *before* the fact—to the same degree to which the historical conditions of progress are demonstrable. For example, it could be demonstrated—and it was demonstrated before the fact—that the French Revolution of 1789 would give, in terms of the historical calculus, a better chance for the development of human freedom than the Ancien Régime. Contrariwise, it could be demonstrated, and was demonstrated long before the fact, that Fascist and National-Socialist regimes would do the exact opposite, namely, necessarily restrict the range of human freedom. Moreover, and I think this is a very important point, such demonstration of the historical *chances* before the fact becomes increasingly rational with the development of our scientific, technical, and material resources and capabilities, with our progress in the scientific mastery of man and nature. The possibilities and contents of freedom today are coming more and more under the control of man: they are becoming increasingly calculable. And with this advance in effective control and calculability, the inhuman distinction between violence and violence, sacrifice and sacrifice becomes increasingly rational. For throughout history, the happiness and freedom, and even the life of individuals, have been sacrificed. If we consider human life *per se* sacred under all conditions, the distinction is meaningless, and we have to admit that history is *per se* amoral and immoral, because it has never respected the sanctity of human life as such. But in fact we do distinguish between sacrifices which are legitimate and sacrifices which are not legitimate. This distinction is an historical one, and with this qualification, ethical standards are also applicable to violence.

Let me now recapitulate and reformulate. In absolute ethical terms, that is to say, in terms of suprahistorical validity, there is no justification for any suppression and sacrifice for the sake of future freedom and happiness, revolutionary or otherwise. But in historical terms we are confronted with a distinction and a decision. For suppression and sacrifice are daily exacted by all societies, and one cannot start—indeed I would like to say this with all possible emphasis—one cannot start becoming moral and ethical at an arbitrary but expedient point of cut off: the point of revolution. Who can quantify and who can compare the sacrifices exacted by an established society and those exacted by its subversion? Are ten thousand victims more ethical than twenty thousand? Such is in fact the inhuman arithmetic of history, and in this inhuman historical context operates the historical calculus. Calculable are the material and intellectual resources available, calculable are the productive and distributive facilities in a society, and the extent of unsatisfied vital needs and of satisfied non-vital needs. Quantifiable and calculable are the quantity and size of the labor force and of the population as a whole. That is the empirical material at the disposal of the historical calculus. And on the basis of this quantifiable material the question can be asked whether the available resources and capabilities are utilized most rationally, that is to say, with a view to the best possible satisfaction of needs under the priority of vital needs and with a minimum of toil, misery and injustice. If the analysis of a specific historical situation suggests a negative answer, if conditions exist in which technological rationality is impeded or even superseded by repressive political and social interests which define the general welfare, then the reversal of such conditions in favor of a more rational and human use of the available resources would also be a maximalization of the chance of progress in freedom. Consequently, a social and political movement in this direction would, in terms of the calculus, allow the presumption of historical justification. It can be no more than a presumption, subject to correction as the movement actually develops, reveals its potential and establishes new facts, or in other words, as it sustains or as it cuts the links between the means which the revolution employs and the end which it professes to attain.

And this leads to the last question which I want to raise here, namely, can the revolutionary end justify *all* means? Can we distinguish between rational and irrational, necessary and arbitrary, suppression? When can such suppression be called rational in terms of the objective of a respective revolution? I shall briefly illustrate the scope of this question by the Bolshevik Revolution. The professed objective of the Bolshevik Revolution was socialism. It implied the socialization of the means of production, the dictatorship of the proletariat as preparatory to a classless society. In the specific historical situation in which the Bolshevik Revolution occurred, socialism called for industrialization in competition with the advanced capitalist countries of the West, for the building up of the armed forces, and for propaganda on a global scale. Now can we apply a distinction between rational and irrational to these objectives and to the degree of suppression involved in them? In terms of the revolution, rational would be accelerated industrialization, the elimination of non-cooperative layers of management from the economy, the enforcement of work discipline, sacrifices in the satisfaction of needs imposed by the priority of heavy industry in the first stages of industrialization, and suspension of civil liberties if they were used for sabotaging these objectives. And we can reject, without long discussion, as not justifiable, even in terms of the revolution, the Moscow trials, the permanent terror, the concentration camps, and the dictatorship of the Party over the working classes. Further examination would require introducing into the discussion the situation of global coexistence; but time forbids us to do so. We have also made abstraction from the human element in the leadership of the revolution, that is to say, from the so-called historical individuals.

And here I want to add one remark. It seems to me characteristic that, the more calculable and the more controllable the technical apparatus of modern industrial society becomes, the more does the chance of human progress depend on the intellectual and moral qualities of the leaders, and on their willingness and ability to educate the controlled population and to make it recognize the possibility, nay, the necessity of pacification and humanization. For today, the technical apparatus of advanced industrial society is in itself authoritarian, requiring service, submission, subordination to the objective mechanism of the machine system, that is to say, submission to those who control the apparatus. Technology has been made into a powerful instrument of streamlined domination—the more powerful the more it proves its efficiency and delivers the goods. And as such, it serves the politics of domination.

I come to the conclusion. The means-end relation is the ethical problem of revolution. In one sense, the end justifies the means, namely, if they demonstrably serve human progress in freedom. This legitimate end, the only legitimate end, demands the creation of conditions which would facilitate and expedite its realization. And the creation of these conditions may justify sacrifices, as it has justified sacrifices throughout history. But this relation between means and ends is a dialectical one. The end must be operative in the repressive means for attaining the end. But no matter how rational, how necessary, how liberating—revolution involves violence. The non-violent history is the promise and possibility of a society which is still to be fought for. At present, the triumphant violence seems to be on the other side.

MORALITY AND IDEOLOGY

Henry David Aiken

HENRY DAVID AIKEN is Professor of Philosophy at Brandeis University. He has also taught at Harvard University, Columbia University and the University of Washington and has been Visiting Professor at the University of Michigan. In 1960–61 he was a Guggenheim fellow. He is a regular contributor to philosophical, literary and popular journals, he has edited *Hume's Moral and Political Philosophy* (1948), *Dialogues Concerning Natural Religion* (1953), and *The Age of Ideology* (1957); he is also the author of *Reason and Conduct* (1962).

I

Since the thirties there has been a general revulsion on the part of liberal intellectuals in the West against all forms of social thought that involve the use of ideological "social myths" for the purpose of organizing and manipulating the attitudes of men. Before the war, this revulsion was reserved mainly for Fascism and Nazism, just as, a century before, it had been reserved for Christianity. After the war, however, owing in part to the decline of Fascism and in part to the break-up of the temporary alliance between the Russians and the Western allies, the sentiment has been focused mainly upon Marxism, and accordingly Marxism has come to be viewed as the paradigm case of an ideology. Unfortunately, there are certain features of Marxist thinking which not only radically distinguish it from Fascism and Nazism, but which show its common origins with liberalism itself. For one thing, although such a doctrine as the withering away of the state may be as mythical as the traditional liberal doctrine of natural law, it was taken no less seriously by Marx and Engels themselves than the latter theory was taken by Locke or Jefferson. No one can doubt that Marx and Engels were taken in by their own theory of history or, indeed, that they considered it quite as realistic and scientific as Newton's principles of mechanics or Darwin's theory of evolution. In fact, Marxism, unlike Fascism and Nazism, is an explicitly antiromantic, rationalistic position which differs from its liberal predecessors, at least by intention, in being more attentive to the historical, material conditions of social change and hence more realistic in its program for the social amelioration of humanity. One main evidence of this rationalism and realism, ironically enough, is Marx's own scornful account of ideology as a misconception of reality which systematically inverts the primordial relation of ideas to being. For Marx, as for the anti-Marxist liberals of our own time, "ideology" connoted, among other things, not only misconception, but systematically misleading misconception, unrealistic and hence ineffectual idealism and utopianism, above all the notion that ideas themselves are, or can be, sources of human liberation.

But there are other ways in which Marx is at once instructive and embarrassing to latter-day liberals of the no-more-ideology school. He is embarrassing because, as most of his commentators concede, Marx was in many ways a child of the Enlightenment, a moralist and man of good will whose own social and political ideals are derived from the same great universalistic principles of liberty, equality, fraternity, and justice which animated the fathers of the French and American Revolutions. So close, indeed, is the underlying ethical ideal of communism to that embodied in the founding documents of the original French and American republics that any thoroughgoing attack upon, or disillusionment with the former is bound to spread, as soon as reflection begins, to the latter as well. And lately it has begun to dawn on some of the more realistic foxes, whose main concern is to protect the existing social system as a going concern, that they have little more use for, or interest in, the *Declaration of Independence* or the *Bill of Rights*, when construed literally and unbendingly as statements of legitimate social and political aspirations to be realized now or in the immediate future, than they do for the *Communist Manifesto* itself. To be sure, they do not openly attack the *Declaration* on street corners (they themselves, it should be understood, do not attack anything on street corners; on the contrary they rather deprecate the whole idea), any more than they denounce the First or the Fifth Amendments in letters to the editor. They are content that the *Declaration*, although not Thoreau's inflammatory and inspiriting essay on civil disobedience, should be read on the Fourth of July, so long at least as it is well understood that the reading of it, like the singing of the Star-Spangled Banner at baseball games, is a collective ritual, a symbolic re-enactment of the original contracting-in which constituted the American people as a nation and its government as a state. To be sure, they neglect the fact that in so doing they themselves are countenancing a mythic, idealistic, frequently misleading use of language as an integral feature of the institutional schemes and practices inherent in, perhaps even definitive of, our social system, our going concern. And they do not realize, or else fail openly to acknowledge that they realize, that they cannot quite mean what they say in calling, as they put it, for an "end to ideology" without at the same time calling for an end to their own conduct as ritual participants in, and presumptive condoners of, a form of expression and a mode of thought which they profess on general grounds to disapprove. Like Marx, they do not really oppose ideology as such but any ideology which threatens the sociopolitical system whose votaries and functionaries they wish to be. Unlike Marx, however, they oppose, on principle, all revolutionary ideologies and honest revolutionary readings of our own ideology.

But, as I have said, there is a form of instruction lodged within this embarrassment, and the anti-ideologists are as thrifty of Marx's example as they are of his ideas. It will be recalled that Marx deplored not only ideology but morality which, for him, was itself merely a kind of ideological sop which, like religion, history has thrown to the weak as a rationalization and pacifier. Of course Marx himself was a practical if disguised moralist, just as he was also a practical, if disguised, ideologist; it was simply more effective in an era of scientism, positivism, and rationalism to pretend to be merely an historian, an economist, and a socialist describing and predicting the course of human events which, happily for the working classes, would just about bring them to the promised land. And in a word, Marx like Jesus was a prophet, that is to say, a successful moralist who employed the language of prediction in order to make his ideals come true. Formally, however, he disdained morality and professed to speak only in realistic and in scientific terms only about class interests and historical events.

Here again the anti-ideological liberals have taken Marx's lesson to heart. Recently, some of them have begun to see that their own across-the-board opposition to ideology is inconsistent with their own public practice. And so, particularly since the demise of the New Frontier, we begin to hear less of the call for an end to ideology and more of an end to that moralistic extremism and radicalism which, often in the name of the *Bill of Rights* and in the language of the *Declaration,* is breaking up not only the supposed consensus of "the great majority of the American people" but in the process destroying the ideological consensualism which the supposed consensus is presumed to embody. And whether the extremists belong, like Mr. Goldwater, to the right of center or, like Dr. King, to the left, they are equally deplored and feared as men of principle. I myself was astonished at the well-nigh universal depreciation of the only memorable utterance of the recent, endless and endlessly dreary campaign. "Let me remind you," cried Mr. Goldwater, "that extremism in the defense of liberty is no vice. And let me remind you also that moderation in the pursuit of justice is no virtue." Here, it seemed to me, was a sentence of which Tom Paine himself might well have been proud. In fact I looked desultorily through the *Rights of Man* to see if Mr. Goldwater were quoting from Paine, since it seemed to me impossible to believe that he could have conceived so splendid and exhilarating a statement of principle all by himself. I did not find it, and I hasten therefore to express my thanks to Mr. Goldwater, and my apologies for momentarily doubting his abilities in this direction. However, to a man, my fellow liberals and fellow neo-pragmatists of the unvital center did not question Mr. Goldwater's sincerity on this occasion; rather did they deplore his thought. Nor did they take issue with his too liberal regard for liberty or his fanatical zeal in behalf of justice, but rather with his moralism as though merely to speak passionately of liberty and justice and of vice and virtue were *infra dig*. And indeed he provided a case study for those who identify morality with visionary extremism and the language of morals itself as a vehicle only for incendiaries, incompetents, or madmen. In short, they regarded Mr. Goldwater's doubtless unconscious reformulation of a part of Aristotle's classical contention about the limitations of the doctrine of the golden mean, not simply as somewhat tactless in the circumstances but rather, in the words of Professor Richard Hofstadter, one of the most distinguished representatives of the anti-ideology school of liberalism, as a "defense of extremism" itself.

As Professor Hofstadter remarks, however, Goldwater is merely the latest and hence the most glaring example of a long line of extremists, or moralists, who from time to time have so rudely tried to upset, and once or twice have succeeded in upsetting, the applecart of the American establishment. To the neo-pragmatic centrists of the end-of-ideology, end-of-morality, end-of-extremism school, morality itself is regarded as an unbending, absolutistic, all-or-nothing code which serves only to mask the outraged resentments of principled malcontents, or else, somewhat less pejoratively, as a ritual form of expression designed at once to legitimate, to authorize, and to mask feelings of inadequacy and incompetence on the part of the so-called moral agent in relation to a system of which he is a faltering, otherwise dangerously resentful, member. In times when there is no clear and present danger to the body politic, the language of morals is a tolerable because relatively harmless way of letting off the steam of social unrest and disaffection. But in times of permanent crisis, such as the whole Western world is now living through, it becomes a dangerous, emotionalistic form of discourse which goads, without guiding, men into extremist positions where abstract rights rather than concrete interests are served and from which unhappy, indignant men make symbolic assaults upon the social system. From this standpoint, America is the happy home of the logroller and the lobbyist, the compromiser and the dealsman, the man of adjustment and accommodation, for whom, not right and wrong, but success, achievement, and expediency are the common terms of practical deliberation and appraisal. Not justice or freedom, but the self-maintenance of the system is—I was about to say —the "good" to be aimed at. And if, on infrequent ceremonial occasions, the anti-moralists permit themselves to use the language of morals, as they also permit themselves to use the language of ideology, it is, or should be, taken for granted by all safe, sane citizens that the language has a little sting but no substance, that, indeed, it is paradoxically merely a ritual out-groupish gesture between members of the in-group which reassures everyone of his essential solidarity with his kind. But really to believe, and hence to act with all one's might upon one's belief, that something is *wrong* in Denmark, really to live, or try to live, up to one's principles as a free moral agent is at best rather to make a nuisance of oneself and at worst to put oneself beyond the pale of our pragmatic, realistic, compromising—and compromised—American system.

Thus conceived, as principled extremism and as a rhetoric of idealistic intemperance and intransigence, moralism and morality are little more than alternate names for ideology, at least as that form of thought is conceived by its contemporary liberal-pragmatic critics. And in fact such a leading anti-ideologist as Professor Daniel Bell has made it quite plain, despite certain incidental murmurs of qualification, that in his view morality is a form of ideology and the moralist himself merely an old-fashioned ideologue who, fortunately for the rest of us, has not yet mastered the more thrilling vocabulary of Marxism. Says Bell, "To see history as changes in sensibilities and style or, more, how different classes or people mobilized their emotional energies and adopted different moral postures is relatively novel; yet the history of moral temper is, I feel, one of the most important ways of understanding social change, and particularly the irrational forces at work in men." Here the moralist is represented as a symbol of irrationalism; elsewhere he is identified as the typical extremist whose significance, however, is symptomatic rather than causal. And one gets the clear impression from Bell's book, *The End of Ideology*, that the very language of morality, like that of ideology, is nothing but a high-sounding but inherently misleading cover for interests which, looked at through eyes undeceived by semantical legerdemain, are as creaturely as any others.

Such a view of morals has, of course, received support for philosophers and psychologists. Some philosophers, deriving in this instance mainly from Nietzsche, represent morality itself as originating in resentment and as being a device employed by the weak in order to bring the strong down to their own level. Others, deriving largely from positivism, contend that the moral judgment is merely an expression of emotions which misleadingly parades itself as an objective ascription of certain properties (goodness, virtue, etc.) to persons, actions, or events. Because it is inherently misleading, devoid of thought, and, where it succeeds in its persuasive effect upon others, is merely a goad to action rather than a rational exposition of cause-effect relationships that leaves us free to decide according to our interest what course of action to choose, morality is at best a dispensable form of verbal magic employed mainly by knaves in order to compel unwitting fools to do what they otherwise would not do—for these and other reasons the free man despises morality and the rational man ignores it. The implication, also more or less explicit in the writings of the anti-ideological school, is that all men require, linguistically for the purposes of conduct, on the one side, a clear, unconfused language for the description and prediction of matters of empirical fact, and on the other, clear, unadorned statements of interest, easily recognizable by anyone for what they are.

The anti-ideologists and anti-moralists thus have, in part, similar axes to grind, though it should be said in fairness that not all anti-ideologists are anti-moralists and vice versa. Thus Bell, in a controversy with the present writer, has claimed, albeit inconsistently, that he never really meant to attack morality itself but only the anti-pragmatic extremist morality of principle which, as in the case of the abolitionists, forces otherwise amiable compromisers into either-or postures of the sort that brought on the acknowledged horrors of the War between the States and the degrading aftermath of the Reconstruction. Conversely, in the case of Nietzsche, for example, there is no direct evidence that his opposition to morality extends also to ideology. On the contrary, he seems at times to hold, with Dostoyevski's Grand Inquisitor, that the "herd" at least must be ruled by non-rational forms of persuasion with which some have identified ideology itself.

II

But it is time that I begin to show my own hand.

In contrast as well as in opposition to the above-mentioned views, I hold that so long as men recognize the significance to themselves of the idea of a first-personal decision-procedure, supported primarily and essentially by the agent's own sense of responsibility and guilt, and by his own conscientious need to atone and redress wrongs, moral discourse will remain as the characteristic vehicle for its expression. For my part, the serious question is not how morality can be transcended or else contained, but rather how the moral agent can become more humane, more imaginative, more sensitive to the whole range of his commitments and relations.

Now it may be supposed from this that I am defending in other terms an archaistic ideology of radical individualism, and that I am merely using a notion of moral discourse as its stalking horse. Such a supposition would be mistaken. As subsequent portions of this paper will make clear, I am concerned to distinguish morality as such from ideology as such in the interests of both.

Let us then give some passing attention to the concepts of morality and of ideology. Now in recent years various attempts by certain linguistic philosophers have been made to represent morality as a formally constituted social institution or discipline or game, whose principles at once define the permissible range of application of the term "moral" and prescribe certain rules of judgment and of action to which all who would speak from *the* moral point of view must conform. From this standpoint, an agent is free, according to his inclination or interest, to opt for or against the moral life but not to decide in conscience what its rules ought to be; once he "contracts into" the moral game, his principles as a moral agent are cut out for him. Nor can it be said that any one ought to play the game of morals, and this for the simple yet compelling reason that the rules of that game define what is to be understood by judgments that prescribe what, in a moral sense, any man ought to do. The moral "ought" thus is alleged to have no significant use outside the game of morals. To be sure, moral agents may disagree—but only, so to say, strategically, not essentially or as a matter of fundamental principle.

Such a view of morality is radically mistaken, not just in detail but in principle. There are a number of arguments which may help to show why this is so. For one thing, this view reduces moral principles to the status of what Kant called "hypothetical imperatives," and in this instance of the sort he described as rules of skill. Hypothetical imperatives prescribe only what we must do, if we are to achieve a certain desired end or result; in this case an end or result which, by hypothesis, is defined by the so-called discipline or activity of morals. But, as Kant himself perceived, moral principles do not present themselves to us in such a fashion. They do not, that is to say, tell us what we must do in order to succeed in a certain sort of play or else what we must do if we are to accomplish a certain result. Quite the contrary, they present themselves, as Kant put it, as categorical imperatives which the moral agent, regardless of inclination, perceives that he ought to fulfill. Further, moral principles are adhered to, not as means to some ulterior end, but for their own sakes as principles. What we do morally, we do, not just on principle, but because of principle. But principles which we follow in this way, quite independently of any ulterior interest which they may serve, cannot be merely hypothetical imperatives, that is to say, principles which we may follow or not follow, according to taste, merely because we happen to be interested in a certain form of activity.

Another way of seeing this is to observe that if there were constitutive or disciplinary principles that laid down the essential conditions of moral competence, it then would become meaningless to inquire whether one ought to adhere to them, since such principles are by definition the principles by which any moral agent is necessarily guided. But it is possible for a person to be morally perplexed about his obligation to *any* principle; that is, it is possible for him to ask whether he himself really ought to judge and act as such a principle prescribes. Indeed, it is possible to ask of any principle which is alleged to define *the* moral point of view, "But ought *I*, after all, to take that point of view?" or "Would it not perhaps be immoral for me to act as that principle prescribes in these circumstances?" But if such a question is morally and hence practically significant, then it cannot be true that there is any supposed principle of morals which I am precluded in good conscience from questioning. On the contrary, conscientious adherence to any principle whatever qualifies me as a moral agent.

Other arguments are possible, but these must here suffice. I conclude then that there is no such thing as a discipline or institution or game of morals although, of course, there is such a thing as moral discipline. Nor is there such a thing as a principle of morals, where the phrase "principle of morals" connotes a disciplinary or constitutive principle of a sort which every competent practitioner of a discipline must know and to which he must submit. Moral principles, rather, are first-personal precepts (I call them preceptive principles) which each moral agent finds that he ought to acknowledge, but which at the same time are categorically binding upon him. Moral freedom is not the freedom to do as you please, but the freedom to decide what sort of person you ought to be. It does not suffice, for moral freedom, that a moral agent should be capable of violating his principles; he must also be capable of deciding for himself what principles he ought to adhere to. And in general, moral principles exist only for men who realize that nothing can prescribe what principles they are to live by but their own consciences.

Morality thus is a form of self-discipline for moral subjects who hold themselves responsible for their actions. This is the grain of truth in Kant's paradoxical contention that the moral agent is a law unto himself. But since, by definition no man can be a law unto himself, it is impossible to view moral principles as laws of any sort. And indeed the very notion of a moral law, like the notion of a moral commandment, is a contradiction in terms. I may, to be sure, follow a certain law or a certain commandment on moral grounds or as a moral principle, but then its serving as a *moral* principle rests upon my conscientious adoption of it, not upon its supposed status as a law or commandment. Hence, the ultimate authority of morality is wholly internal, never external. And, as I have argued elsewhere, the objectivity which is normally acknowledged by the moral agent or judge as binding upon him is itself only another moral precept which prescribes how he ought to think; it does not state a formal condition to which any putative moral judgment must submit if it is to stand as a moral principle.

In certain circumstances morality ceases to exist as a form of thought and life. Where individuals live unremorsefully and beyond self-reproach, moral decisions and actions are impossible. It is senseless to speak of an action, however unattractive or revolting to ourselves, as morally wrong if the person who performed it is incapable of self-reproach for its performance or has no sense of obligation to make amends. In short, morality cannot exist where there is no sense of personal guilt and hence no sense of personal responsibility for one's conduct toward others. And where such a sense is absent moral judgment has no purchase and the language of moral blame or praise is merely idling.

Let me now say something about the concept of ideology. Here I can do little more than to present the distillate of a theory of ideology to which I have come rather slowly and which has been more adequately developed in other writings. Now, if ideology were to be conceived, as the anti-ideologists think it should, in essentially pejorative terms as an inherently fantastic or misleading utopian, or revolutionary, form of thought, it would of course follow trivially and uninterestingly that morality, which demands above all personal self-awareness, integrity, and virtue, must be opposed to ideology with all its heart and mind. Again, if ideology were by nature spiritually corrupting or enslaving, it would also follow, unilluminatingly, that the moral agent must automatically condemn the ideologist as a kind of pervert, bent on turning the language of conduct into an instrument of power for the manipulation of spiritual robots that have no consciences to call their own. Such a view of ideology, although, as we have seen, still widely held both in this country and in England, does grave injustice to many of the ideological systems through which honest and decent men have sought to establish various forms of cohesive social, cultural, and political life. Worse, it imbues those who accept it with a general, indiscriminate disdain for a very wide range of discourses as well as of the forms of social action animated and ordered by them. In this sphere what is wanted, rather, is discrimination and choice, based upon understanding, among particular discourses and activities within the range called ideological. And this is impossible until built-in pejorative associations have been eliminated from the concept.

As I conceive it, then, an ideology is to be understood in terms of its active function or role as a determinant of one's general comportment as the member of a social group. If, by a "way of life," one means not just a series of individual choices or decisions, but a more or less authoritative and comprehensive frame by means of which the members of a social group, conceived as members, organize their major activities, then an ideology may be taken to represent, whether in part or in whole, a social way of life. It is, so to say, the controlling conceptual frame for such a way of life.

It should be understood, however, that, like the British Constitution, ideologies are not always written down. Moreover, when attempts are made to formulate and to codify them, some changes of content as well as some shifts of meaning or emphasis usually result. On the other hand ideologies may originate in writings, and these of very different sorts. For example, the writings of Locke and Rousseau, of Byron, of Calvin and Joseph Smith, of Newton, Darwin, and Freud all have had immense ideological significance in addition to their characteristic value as philosophy, poetry, theology, or empirical science. It cannot be too often insisted that the ideological character of a proposition cannot be determined exclusively either by an analysis of its purely logical content or by a determination of its traditional literary genre. What is required also is a study of its use in context as a determinant of the activities, the energies of a social group. Accordingly, propositions which function ideologically in one context may not do so in another; or they may, in some circumstances, function in several ways at the same time. Generally speaking, ideological propositions are of two main sorts: (a) propositions that articulate goals, ideals, standards of justification, rules of legitimation, validation, and verification; these I call "ideological leading principles"; and (b) propositions (I sometimes call them "overbeliefs") that provide supporting contexts of belief concerning the nature of the world, man's place in it, the nature and condition of man himself, his history and institutions, and, not least, the major categorial bases of interpretation through which various forms of thought and expression are, and are to be, construed and interrelated; and all of these I refer to as "ideological principles of orientation." Obviously, I do not mean to draw a hard or fast line between leading principles and principles of orientation. Still less do I assume that they exemplify two essentially distinct modes of meaning. On the contrary, I have rather deliberately precluded such a way of distinguishing them by placing what I have called principles of interpretation in the second, rather than the first, group.

Now an "ideology" may be grandly metaphysical or profoundly religious, when it addresses itself to a whole way of life and to a whole notion of what is significant or valuable. But it is also possible to speak more narrowly of the ideology of an institution, an art, or even a cultural style. In the latter instance, the ideology will articulate the ends aimed at by the institution; usually, however, it will also tend to place those ends in relation to other ends and against a background of pertinent overbeliefs. There may therefore be total ideologies, but there may also be special ideologies. And of course special ideologies may themselves be applications or adaptations of total ideologies to the special circumstances involved in particular institutional activities or concerns.

It should be emphasized here that although an ideology may originate in philosophy, it differs from a philosophy in so far as the latter answers exclusively to the queries and concerns of particular individuals. An ideology always represents a point of view which is interpersonal; it also purports to be more or less impersonal and objective. To speak ideologically, therefore, is never to engage in pure *tête à tête*.

If I speak to you ideologically, I speak to you as, say, a liberal, a communist, a Catholic, a democrat, a proletarian, or a scholar, or, in certain circumstances, as a man. When I speak to you yourself, directly, whatever you are, whoever you are, in your whole being, leaving it up to you to respond or not to respond to what I say, simply for yourself, then I speak to you personally and as a philosopher. This does not mean, let me again insist, that ideological addresses are fraudulent or inauthentic. For, of course, all of us acknowledge ourselves to be members of various groups and to have responsibilities which pertain to us if only in some capacity or role. Ideological discourses are fraudulent only when they purport to address us in our nakedness as individuals yet endeavor to shame us, in one way or another, as, say, fathers and mothers, Americans, democrats, Jews, or, most subtly and devastatingly, as members of what Hume called "the party of humanity." An ideology may avail itself of social sanctions, in Bentham's sense, in order to make itself felt; but if it conceals this fact, the philosopher is bound to expose it.

Now it is my impression that most people, much of the time, think and act in ideological terms. And this is no less true of Protestants than of Catholics, no less true of democrats than of communists, no less true of atheists than of Knights of Columbus. However, most of us occasionally and a few of us frequently think and act in terms that are not ideological or at any rate are not purely ideological. Hence, if I appear to represent morality and ideology as contrasting ways of life, or of the moral agent and the ideologue as conflicting persons, I shall seriously misrepresent the position I am trying to develop. Actually, even when we engage in what are first-personal philosophical discussions, seeking a wisdom of life, in the first instance, simply for ourselves, a wisdom with which to face our own existences and fates, we are likely to find that our thinking moves in and out of certain ideological views of things which we ourselves have adopted and which, for one reason or another, we have taken to our hearts. What we initially accept from an ideological point of view, as functionaries, as members of a group or of a kind, including something called human kind, we may, like Albert Camus, reaffirm simply as Albert Camus. I fancy, in fact, that a great part of that dialogue of the soul with itself which Socrates celebrated is a dialogue between the person and a variety of ideological personae. The mistake is to assume that the dialogue is ever closed or that those who take part in it must never be permitted to change their places.

III

I wish now to examine, all too briefly and schematically, certain interesting dialectical relationships between morality and ideology. To this end, let me introduce two parallel distinctions, first between the moral agent, or man of conscience as I shall sometimes call him, and the moralist, and then between the ideologue, or agent of some ideology, and the ideologist.

By a moral agent, or man of conscience, I mean of course simply any individual in his daily activity of trying, according to his lights, to determine what he ought to do in his dealings with other persons, what principles he should try to live by, and how he ought to comport himself toward the otherwise non-moral or extra-moral enterprises that impinge upon his moral concerns, and hence create for him genuine problems of moral choice. On the other hand, the moralist, as I conceive him here, is one whose concern is to understand morality and, so to say, to represent it at that court of reason where philosophical critiques are supposedly conducted. When he performs his role systematically and with a view to all the limiting questions which the moral agent may raise, the moralist of course becomes by stages the moral philosopher. My concern here, however, is not directly with the moral philosopher who, just because he is a philosopher, must have already moved beyond the perspectives afforded by morality alone, but simply the moralist whose whole loyalty is to the moral agent. In passing it is worth emphasizing that the moral agent, not the moralist, is the fundamental moral reality; moralists and moral philosophers, however valuable their services, always ride piggy-back on his shoulders. They can make sense in the end only to the extent that he already has made a sense for them to examine and to represent. Accordingly they should keep their place and not try, as some moralists have done, to usurp his role and hence to give to morality a bad name which should be reserved for bad moralists and moral philosophers.

By analogy, an ideologue is one who, like the original ideologues of France or like the Marxists, the Fascists, or the liberal democrats, advocates and represents some particular ideology. Any ideologue always faces other ideologues as a partisan. His role, therefore, is not to explain or defend ideology, but only to employ the forms and resources of ideological discourse or action in making his ideological commitments prevail. By an ideologist, on the other hand, is to be understood, by analogy with the moralist, one whose role is to explain and to represent ideology at the philosophical court of reason.[1]

---

[1] By a series of obvious inversions we may envisage the pure anti-ideologist who opposes, or professes to oppose, ideology as a form of thought and of life, as well as the anti-moralist as one who opposes the whole notion of personal moral activity, including moral judgment, justification, and agency and who, if he could, would root out the whole complex of moral sentiments, including, for example, indignation, guilt, gratitude, and respect. The immoralist, however, is a more difficult and elusive notion. For present purposes it may suffice to define the immoralist as a moral agent who, on principle, systematically acts against the moral principles of persons with whom he stands ordinarily in close and permanent moral relations. Thus, for example, the concept of the anti-moralist emerges fairly clearly in some of the writings of Nietzsche and, on some interpretations, in those of Freud, whereas that of the immoralist is perhaps best exemplified in the work of such writers as André Gide. I know of no established term for the ideologue who, by analogy to the immoralist, seeks systematically to undermine an ideology accepted by a group of persons with whom he is deeply and permanently involved and whose affairs are of constant concern to him. For the sake of discussion I shall call him simply a

What I wish first to consider now are the relations between the moralist and the ideologist in their own somewhat abstract confrontations. Now it seems to me plain enough that the moralist cannot oppose ideology as such on the grounds that it is prone to irrationalism, that it involves the use of myths or appeals to supernatural authorities, or that it is extremist or utopian. For some forms of ideology do not exemplify these characteristics; moreover, some forms of moral thought do exemplify them. There are ideological extremists such as the Populists who are prepared to sacrifice every other social or political end to the will of the many. But there are also ideological moderates such as James Madison who seek a social system that balances the will of the many against the need for a rule of law and the passion for liberty against the need for security and social justice. Likewise, there are moral extremists, who, like Antigone, would sacrifice every other right or good upon the altar of a particular principle. But there are moral compromisers who, like Aristotle, defend on principle the principles of adjustment and reconciliation. Thus the tension between the moralist and the ideologist must be located elsewhere.

Now there is a great passage in the first chapter of G. E. Moore's *Principia Ethica* which, as it seems to me, provides a clue to what we are looking for. In summarizing his objections to the tendency of ethical naturalists (as he calls them) to define moral goodness in terms of some objective property that is, or is alleged to be, common to morally good things, Moore goes beyond the point which he has hitherto been making, namely, that the naturalist is guilty of the logical error of confusing distinct ideas, to the new and extremely important contention that the tendency to identify moral

---

counter-ideologue. Now it seems to me, that in some veins Gabriel Marcel and Martin Buber and perhaps Albert Camus may be viewed as genuine anti-ideologists, whereas most representatives of the end-of-ideology school in America and England are not anti-ideologists but counter-ideologues who do not fully understand the nature of their own position.

goodness as such with some prevailing standard or criterion of moral goodness, some factor or property of things which is, or may be thought to make them good, can also be a source of grave moral error. Thus, says Moore, "If we start with the conviction that a definition of good can be found, we start with the conviction that good *can mean* nothing else than some one property of things; and our only business will then be to discover what that property is. But if we recognize that, so far as the meaning of good goes, anything whatever may be good, we start with a much more open mind." I myself am not suggesting, as Moore seems to be doing here, that the individual moral agent himself must be an advocate of the open mind. The advocate of extreme open-mindedness in morals represents a particular moral point of view which could easily lead to moral skepticism and paralysis of the will. However, Moore's statement supplies the text for a very different thesis, namely that the kind of extreme open-mindedness which Moore himself apparently advocates here is at least morally possible. If this thesis is correct, as I believe it to be, then the moralist, as an advocate of the moral life, is bound to defend a form of life that *makes* such open-mindedness possible. In short, the moralist is defending, among other things, not the obligation of the moral agent to keep his infernal open question "but is it good?" going in the face of all difficulties including possible alienation from all of his peers, but his prerogative to do so. And in defending this prerogative, this moral possibility, he is bound on principle to be suspicious of the tendency inherent in any ideology, liberal as well as illiberal, to require of its devotees unquestioning submission to its own creed. A liberal ideology may be as individualistic as you please; but, as an ideology, it is to that extent hostile to any moral agent who questions whether he ought to adhere to its premises. And, in short, the moralist, concerned as he is to defend the prerogatives of first-personal moral judgment and decision, and hence the fundamentality of purely first-personal relations and first-personal responsibilities among men, is bound to be hostile to the tendency of every ideologue to adopt the impersonal tone of the functionary and the official spokesman, even when the latter speaks as an exponent of something called "the free society," "democratic liberalism," or "the rule of law." Again, every ideologue, just because he represents an orthodoxy to which he is committed as the member of a class or group, is bound to resent precisely those limiting questions which even the most sympathetic moral agent, in no name but his own, is capable of raising. Hence, the moralist who, for his part, is bound to defend such questions, as well as the prerogatives, the self-constituting and self-construed authority of him who raises them, will inevitably be suspicious of any ideologue, however liberal or open-ended the point of view he represents, who as an ideologue, is bound impersonally to censure any member of his party who, peremptorily and without a by-your-leave, raises the ancient first-person scruple, "But after all is said and done, ought I really to be all that liberal and open-minded in my thought and action?" It is, in short, the orthodoxy of the ideologue, not the principles which he orthodoxly adheres to, which the moralist must resent. And it is precisely this resentment which even the orthodox liberal finds it so hard to understand or to forgive. "In God's name," we can hear him cry, "what does the moralist want that we liberals are not prepared to grant his blasted moral agent?" And to this the moralist can only reply, "Nothing really, except acknowledgment of the possibility that the moral agent, the man of conscience may seriously ask whether after all liberalism may be wrong, and thus to treat himself in relation to liberalism as, in principle, an independent moral agent and critic."

The moralist, it should be understood, is not necessarily defending subjectivism as against objectivism. The ordinary moral agent, as I have tried to show elsewhere, is by no means a principled subjectivist; on the contrary, he has his own conscientious way of being, or trying to be objective, through reconsideration and sober second thought. But objectiv*ism*, which precludes the very possibility of untrammeled first-personal reconsideration and appraisal, is inherent in every form of ideological thought, no matter how liberal may be its principles. The ideologue, even at his most visionary and utopian, never speaks merely for his own visions but always in behalf of a group; he never gives us simply his own sober second thoughts, never tells us simply what he, as a person, considers to be right or good or true or beautiful. And in a word, it is not the objectivity of the ideologue which the moralist may seem to oppose, but his objectivism. And what makes him uneasy in the presence of all ideological discourse is the incessant, impersonal drone of the establishmentarian, the representative man, the wholly public personage.

On the other side, the ideologist is as naturally and properly suspicious of the very conscientiousness of the moral agent who, in reserving his judgment or his question, makes it clear that he cannot be absolutely trusted as the member of any party, however splendid its cause, or the absolute adherent to any orthodoxy, however ancient its lineage. What galls the ideologist in the case of Socrates is not that he has gone whoring after false or foreign gods but that he has his own daemon, not his opinions, but his opinionatedness, his presumption of a right or an obligation to stand alone even against the liberal, democratic orthodoxy of the *polis*. Again, what worried the spokesmen of the ancient regime in the case of Voltaire was not so much his social and political opinions as his presumption of a duty to offer them on his own. The French ideologues regarded him as a cultural hero; yet they would have found him, just as the Athenians found Socrates, a thorn in their flesh. The moralist must find something reassuring and refreshing, something incomparably choice, in a Thoreau. But the ideologist is bound to regard Thoreau as, at best, a kind of fool, absurdly going his own way even when he has, really, nowhere to go, and at worst as a kind of symbol of the unsafe, the untrustworthy, unrepresentative man who refuses to pay his taxes just to prove a point. What gravels the ideologist in a word is not the objective behavior, the substantive public acts of the Thoreaus of the world, most of whom, of course, are harmless enough, but simply the fact that they have consciences of their own.

IV

At this point I can imagine that some one will exclaim, as did the reader of an earlier version of this paper, "But don't you see? You yourself have destroyed ideology. The ideologist is a golem, a pure example of the organization man who believes in organization for its own sake and at all costs. The moralist, whatever his faults, is defending the little fellow, the individual person. In an age of ideologies, he represents the spirit of the resistance which you yourself have often extolled. He is the original, final enemy of totalitarianism, of the soul-destroying collective in which all independence and all personal freedom is lost." There is power in this criticism. Can anything be said in reply?

Let us recall our distinctions between the ideologist and the ideologue and the moralist and the moral agent, the man with a conscience. The man with a conscience is not called upon to defend something called morality at all costs; nor is he bound *a priori* to be a moralist. Suppose now we take another look at the moralist, against his own protests, from an ideological point of view. Who, among the varieties of ideologue, is his counterpart? I think the answer is plain. He is the absolute anarchist, the utopian counter-ideologue who, abstractly and on principle, despises and condemns the bureaucrat, the functionary, the organization man and the forms of life generally associated with the social system. In a word, he is the ideologue to end all ideologues. Americans are traditionally and sentimentally attracted to such a figure. He is the Henry David Thoreau of *Civil Disobedience* and *Walden;*

he is also Huckleberry Finn, the Outcast of Poker Flat, the Lone Ranger, and a thousand and one other free spirits that live out of time, out of history, in the literary imagination.

Let us recall also that the actual moral agent finds himself, as is and in context, bound by certain particular moral judgments and decisions. Regardless of his inclination, like you or me, he finds, willy-nilly, that he has assumed certain responsibilities and, accordingly, that he *ought* to fulfill them. Or else he perceives that he has failed to do what he should have done and so is in conscience bound to make amends. His commitment is to what, according to his conscience, he finds to be right, not to an abstract idea entitled "morality." It is not difficult to conceive a moral agent, a man of conscience, who finds himself, as matters stand, profoundly committed to certain historical institutional practices or activities, such as a rule of law or a bill of rights, and to the covering ideological traditions that have been their doctrinal shields. Nor is it hard to imagine that such a person might find it simply frivolous, in a situation where such traditions and practices are under systematic and continual attack, merely to represent the moralist, that is to say, the ahistorical anarchist who is so obsessed by the idea of the *tête à tête*, the dialogical, or I-Thou, relationship that he ignores the only historical institutions that, in reality, have enabled such relationships to exist. The historical Socrates, be it recalled, elected to stay in Athens and to submit to the verdict of the ideologues, the functionaries, the public men who had condemned him to death.

My conclusion is this. Few men of good will, when they examine their consciences, can condemn the ideologue out of hand. The ideologue may not be loveable; undoubtedly he is a tedious dinner companion. But if the ideology which he professes is, on the whole, beneficent and will, in practice, serve the cause of peace and the amelioration of the lot of the great masses of suffering humanity, I will take him any time in preference to the moralist whose only concern is the good conscience itself. There are ideologies and ideologies, some bad, some indifferent, a few useful. Ideologies, like other forms of life, are as they do. And by their fruits so should we judge them. Meanwhile, we have our consciences to live with as we can in an age of perpetual crisis in which each of us is faced with moral problems of unprecedented difficulty, and the whole world is confronted with tasks of ideological reconstruction and creation which will not be finished for many generations.

UTILITY AND MORAL REASONING

A. I. Melden

A. I. MELDEN is Professor and Chairman of the Department of Philosophy at the University of California in Irvine. He has held Ford Foundation and Guggenheim fellowships and served as president of the Pacific Division of the American Philosophical Association (1961–62). He has contributed to many anthologies and has written widely on questions of ethics, freedom, philosophical psychology and human rights. He is the editor of *Ethical Theories* (1955) and of *Essays in Moral Philosophy* (1958), and the author of *Rights and Right Conduct* (1959) and of *Free Action* (1961).

The view that conduct is ultimately justified only by its utility remains, despite the admittedly formidable objections that have been directed against it, a live doctrine. And rarely do its defenders risk intemperance by dismissing the objections to it as vestiges of everyday confusion, superstition or irrationality. Why then should the doctrine in one form or another continue to claim vigorous champions? Our thinking cannot be sound if it represents as a mere slip of the intellect an incorrect view so persistently held. We need to understand not only that it is wrong but also why it should have been thought right.

I shall consider one test case, the obligation of promises. I shall begin by stating an extreme form of the doctrine, the one commonly called "act-utilitarianism" in order to exhibit, briefly, its failure to deal with this case. I shall then consider certain so-called rule-utilitarianisms, and I shall argue that in all of them what is overlooked or misunderstood is the moral

context within which utility operates as a justifying consideration and within which, too, the promise is intelligible as an
obligation-creating act. If this is so, then the appeal to utility
presupposes but cannot itself elucidate the moral matters it
is designed to explain. It is this familiar neglect of context
that, while intelligible, is fatal to the various forms of utilitarian theory.

I

By "act-utilitarianism" is meant the view that the necessary
and sufficient condition of the rightness of any particular act
is that it maximizes a good that is thought to be wholly present in individual experiences and is usually identified with
pleasure or the satisfaction of desire. Now on the very face of
it, the substitution of the principle "Maximize pleasure!" for
the variety of moral principles or rules by which we are in
fact guided in our conduct, poses serious difficulties for act-
utilitarianism. I shall not dwell here upon the familiar problem of distribution that can only bring into question the allegation that the maximizing of good is sufficient ground of
right conduct: there is no contradiction involved in the conception of an act that maximizes the goods of satisfactions or
pleasures only by saddling a class of social scapegoats with
the burden of evil. And the fact, if it is a fact, that this does
not or cannot happen is a function of just those features for
which no provision is allowed in this monolithic theory, the
moral concern of persons with each other as human beings
endowed with rights and the impossibility, given this context
or mutual moral regard, that such persons can remain indifferent to social injustice. Rather, I want to focus attention at
this point upon the consideration that is due those to whom
we stand in quite special moral relations, and the immediate
implication of this fact, namely, that the maximizing of the
goods of experience is not even a necessary condition of right
conduct.

For, we are not only human beings endowed with rights to be safeguarded in the interests of social justice, but specific persons—husbands or wives, parents of offspring, persons who have given our word and now have promises to keep. A good doing that ignores the special obligations incurred by promising, the special obligations involved in such social positions or the special obligation to guard against the punishment of the innocent, is an indiscriminate and irresponsible do-gooding. Hence the familiar counterexamples urged against act-utilitarianism: the wrong-doing involved in the punishment of the innocent; or in the flouting of one's solemn word, each of which may be eminently useful in special circumstances. And in fact we are called upon not infrequently to choose between the keeping and the breaking of a promise when we do reasonably judge that we ought to keep the promise with *no* assurance that the promise-keeping act will maximize pleasures or satisfactions. For who knows what will be the future consequences of every promise-keeping act, for all time and for all persons and perhaps too for all other sentient creatures—why exclude animals if they too can share in pleasant and painful or unpleasant experience? And if one had to choose, given the assurance (however reached) that no increase in such goods would be secured by keeping one's promise, we should still have a good reason for doing so, namely, that it would be a case of keeping one's promise. But on act-utilitarian doctrine this conviction can be put down only as irrational, as due to the inertia of blind habit. For, on that doctrine, one is to keep one's word or anything else you please, deliberately and rationally, if and only if by doing so one maximizes good. And this is bizarre.

II

The trouble with act-utilitarianism is its failure to recognize that our ordinary rules, principles or maxims, whether these be about promise-keeping or truth-telling or the protection of the innocent, pose considerations which, if applicable, are always and necessarily relevant to the determination of what one should do. It is not that one ought to keep one's promise if doing so maximizes good, but that one ought to do so. The rule is not iffy. But this, it has been held, implies not the rejection, but only the application elsewhere, of the principle of utility. For the trouble with act-utilitarianism, it has been argued, is that it applies the principle at the wrong place, to particular acts. A particular act is to be justified only by appealing to the general rule, but, with one exception to be noted later, it is only the rule to which utility applies. Thus restricted (hence the term "rule-utilitarianism") utility is "the sole foundation of morals."

But this is much too vague. An act-utilitarian might well concede on purely tactical grounds that we are not to appeal to utility in our justification of particular acts. Time is too short for any of us, and knowledge and intelligence are too limited for most, if not all of us, to permit us to consider the consequences of everything we do. It is eminently useful, therefore, that we rely not on utility but on our common moral rules; for experience has taught us the utility of ignoring utility and of depending upon such guidance. An act-utilitarian might then agree that in our deliberations we are to be guided, as a matter of moral tactics, by our everyday moral rules while insisting that what alone justifies our performances is their utility. Such a view is not self-contradictory, however offensive it might be, in recommending that we ignore in our deliberations just these considerations—the goods and ills our doings bring to pass—which alone would justify our conduct.

Equally, it is consistent with act-utilitarianism to argue, as Hume did, that we are not to judge a particular act on the basis of its special features, but to be guided by general rules. Returning food stolen by the destitute from persons who have no need of it, is right, according to Hume, even though doing this may be harmful to the former and useless to the latter. For it is shortsighted, Hume argued, to ignore the oblique effect of such acts in preserving the stability of the eminently useful rules of possession. So it would be shortsighted to argue for the merit of an act of promise-breaking on the grounds of its utility while ignoring the unfortunate effect of that act upon the rule of promises in weakening the general confidence that promises will be kept. On act-utilitarian grounds Hume argued that no exceptions to moral rules are to be allowed, thus matching Kant, albeit for very different reasons, in his most uncompromising moralistic mood.

The case is not materially different in Mill's account of moral reasoning, although here there is a more realistic appreciation of the fact that an agent is sometimes obliged to decide between competing moral rules. On Mill's view, moral rules are corollaries of the supreme principle of morality, that is, experience has demonstrated the utility of our ordinary moral rules. Since it is only in this way that one is justified in being guided by them, the justification of any particular act is to be given, when fully spelled out, in terms of its utility. Certainly it would be an arbitrary verbal stipulation, not open to Mill himself, to restrict the application of the expression "moral justification" to cases in which rules are cited as grounds for our doings, since Mill expressly allows that, where competing moral rules apply, our only resort is to appeal directly to utility in order to resolve our moral dilemmas. Mill's utilitarianism turns out to be indistinguishable in principle from the act-utilitarianism of old.

Two connected and fatal ideas run through the doctrine. *Prima facie* there are many sorts of consideration that serve morally to justify conduct, but in point of fact there is only utility. And this brings into question the whole character of our ordinary moral thinking not only by questioning whether the manifold considerations which, commonly, we offer in justification of our conduct are valid reasons but also by substituting something for them which does not strike us as a moral reason at all. If one does something because it is pleasant or enjoyable for all concerned, that no doubt is a reason for doing it; but the view that this is a *moral* reason, and the only one to boot, runs counter to our moral sensibilities. And this is vouched for by the familiar counterexamples to classical utilitarian theory: the morally objectionable but useful and hence, on utilitarian theory, justified flouting of a solemn promise (or the morally offensive but useful punishment of the innocent—the examples can be multiplied) in which, if it is performed in perfect secrecy and promptly and completely forgotten or cast out of everybody's mind, none of the disturbing inutility that usually attends such acts need arise.

If rule-utilitarianism is to be distinguishably different in principle from act-utilitarianism, it must somehow rule out as inadmissible in principle the attempt to justify particular acts in terms of their utility. And it must declare that an act prescribed by a moral rule, for example, a promise-keeping act, is *as such* and not derivatively, because of its contingent utility, a good action to perform. If utility is to enter the picture at all its role must be restricted to the reasons, necessarily non-moral, that warrant the adoption of our everyday rules.

III

One attempt to meet these specifications is to be found in Stephen Toulmin's view.[1] It is one thing, he tells us, to justify an action in terms of an accepted practice and it is another to justify the practice. Questions about the rightness of an action are resolved by determining whether or not the action conforms to the practice where the practice is what is done in our society in conformity with certain recognized rules. Questions about the "justice" of a given practice are questions which go beyond the moral code, for the moral code *is* the accepted practice. Such questions are not strictly speaking moral questions; they are questions of utility and if they pertain to practices sufficiently complex in their ramifications (e.g., the institution of marriage), they raise questions con-

[1] *The Place of Reason in Ethics* (Cambridge, 1950).

cerning our whole way of life and can be settled only on the basis of personal preference or decision. In matters of morality, strictly speaking, we are concerned with the harmonizing of the actions of persons, and for this only the done thing, that is, the accepted practice as specified by rules, is relevant, except in cases of competing rules where we are obliged to decide on the basis of utility. But if there is only one applicable rule, the moral justification can consist only in a reference to the accepted practice specified by it. In such cases it is not that it is undesirable to appeal to utility; it is logically absurd to do so.

In this view we find the first of the recently fashionable distinctions between justifying an action in terms of a practice and justifying the practice as a practice. And, as in the case of other writers who draw this distinction, there is something in this talk about practices vaguely reminiscent of Wittgenstein's references to the language-game, to "this is what we do"—but with a very considerable difference. For here the reference to a practice is the reference to the done thing not, as in Wittgenstein's talk about language-games, in order to elucidate a concept by exhibiting the ways in which, within the context of practical activities, discourse plays its communicative role, but in order to establish the truth of the proposition that an action is justified, by showing that it is the done thing and thus harmonizes or fits in, in some useful way, with the actions of others.

Why then would it be impermissible to offer utility as a moral reason for a particular action? The answer is not the verbal one that this is not what we *call* a "moral reason." It is to be found, rather, in the conception of morality as a matter pertaining to the ways in which conformity in behavior enables persons to "harmonize" their actions, to get along with one another in ways which depend crucially upon the predictable (because customary) behavior of others. Hence the frequent analogies drawn by Toulmin with incidents on the road: "If . . . I am asked why I was driving on the *left*, the only answer I can give is that the left-hand side is the one on which one does drive in England—that the Rule of the Road *is* to drive on the left," and, "Suppose that I am driving along a winding country road and deliberately keep on the left-hand side going round the blind corners. . . . My care to keep to the left remains 'right,' my decision not to take any risks on the corners remains 'correct,' in spite of the fact that the consequences in exceptional cases might well be unfortunate."[2] Here the utility of the practice depends upon the fact that this is the practice—nothing more—the recognized and established way in which one does it. There is no more intrinsic merit in driving on the right than on the left, and provided everyone or nearly everyone drives on the left in England and anywhere else, that would be good enough reason for you and for me to follow suit. If morality is a matter of "harmonizing" actions—if this is our moral purpose—what more effective way can there be than by conforming, by doing the done thing?

Effective it may well be. But, desirable? That, surely, is quite another question; and it is one that can be raised about any practice. But if morality is a social arrangement whose function it is simply to "harmonize" actions, then no smoothly efficient social arrangement, however integral to its operations its gas ovens for an unwanted minority may be, is in principle subject to moral criticism. To be sure, morality does enable us to carry on working relations with one another, but in ways that involve far more than a matter of what is done as a rule or what we make it a rule to do. For unlike a matter of social habit or custom or any social arrangement from which we may retreat or not as we choose, morality is a way of life and all that this implies: it involves not only doing but also thinking and caring and hoping and wishing and feeling, in ways that are involved in the moral understanding we have of others and ourselves. The roots of morality go deep, into our very status as the human beings we are; they do not lie on the surface in the devices, instruments, habits and customs

[2] Toulmin, *loc. cit.*, p. 145.

we may or may not adopt or follow, in order that the actions of each of us, by being regularized and rendered predictable, might "harmonize" with those of others. We need here consider the implications of the view only for the obligation of promises to be assured of this point.

We are told that the fact that something was promised is a good reason for doing what one promised to do, and so far so good. But if we ask why it is a good reason, why indeed after citing the fact that a promise was made, the question "Why ought . . . ?" cannot arise, the only answer we find is that "there is no more general 'reason' to be given beyond one which relates the action in question to an accepted social practice."[3] Viewed in this light, a promise is a social device employed by two parties, each of which, normally, gains something from the other, one immediately upon uttering the words "I promise . . . ," the other at some future date. But this account of the practice of promising is curiously bereft of just that feature of the promise that is essential to it, namely, the obligation it creates. For if the promise is the sort of practice described above—I say "I promise . . . ," and later consider doing the thing which, as *we* put it, I promised to do—why indeed *should* I go on to do it? Surely the fact that this is the practice of others is of no matter to me unless I want to do the done thing. Nor is the fact that doing the done thing is useful to all who participate relevant unless I am concerned with what is useful to others; if not, not. If I understand the transaction in this way it is clear that I do not understand *what* a promise is and in consequence *that* I have promised—all that I understand is that there is a curious general practice involving the utterance of the words "I promise . . ." and that, for no good reason that I can determine, people engage in it in a quite particular way. This, indeed, is precisely what very young children, before they grasp the import of the performance, do understand. But so regarded no provision is made for what is essential to promising,

[3] *Ibid.*

namely, the fact that the person uttering the words "I promise . . ." places himself under an obligation. And it is this fact—that by promising one assumes an obligation and not that by uttering certain words a person engages in a customary practice—which provides the justification for the subsequent promise-keeping action.

What then is missing in this account of the obligation of promises? Surely it is precisely that background of moral understanding and trust which any moral philosophy must acknowledge and elucidate, and in the absence of which the promise locution could not possibly do its work as the declaration that the person to whom it is addressed can depend or count upon, or expect, the performance described. For to depend or count upon, or to expect, the act is not merely to reckon with confidence that a certain event will occur, whether because of intention, resolution or habit, or public custom or practice (although sometimes we do speak ironically of depending or counting upon someone to act out of habit, lust, folly or because of social or legal pressure). It is, rather, to trust him as a person who, in promising, has placed his credit as a responsible human being on the line and tied it to the promised act, and who might well risk, as a consequence of failure, some measure of the disapproval, distrust, suspicion, opprobrium or even fear that we reserve for those with whom the ties of moral understanding have in varying degrees weakened or broken down.[4] It is this moral context and all that is involved in thought and feeling no less than in the "predictable" or "regularized" externals of conduct, that is missing in this talk about justifying an act in terms of a practice and in this account of past promises as reasons for present doings.

[4] Cf. my article "On Promising," *Mind*, LXV (1956).

IV

How can rule-utilitarianism, while maintaining its distinctive restriction of utility to moral rules, do justice to just those obligations that pose difficulties for the older utilitarianism? If a promise *as such* is a reason for the doing promised, then the connection between the promise and the obligation it creates must be conceptual and not contingent upon the matter-of-fact but conceivably alterable course of nature. Conspicuously, this has long been recognized by philosophers from Hobbes on down to other non-utilitarians of the present day. For the supposition that one has promised but is under no obligation at all is self-contradictory. The rule-utilitarianism to which I shall now turn attempts to explain this conceptual connection by offering us an altogether novel view of the nature of moral rules.

On the older views of Hume and Mill, the notion of a promise was thought to be intelligible independently of the moral rule that one ought to keep one's promises. Indeed, a promise was thought by Hume to be "a form of words," that is, a ceremonial utterance, by which one person signifies to another his intention of performing a given act, thereby arousing an expectation in the other so that, in the event of failure, he exposes himself to censure of some sort. The fact that this account is at least inadequate, for so far we do not have a promise at all or the obligation created by it, is one of the skeletons in Hume's own closet. For if this is promising, then promising no more obliges than any other act by which intentionally one creates expectations in others of what one will do in the future. Our common sense that necessarily a promise obliges was put down by Hume to a queer fiction of the imagination,[5] and, by other utilitarians, to downright con-

[5] *A Treatise of Human Nature*, Bk. III, Pt. II, Sec. 5 ("Of the Obligation of Promises").

fusion. According to all such thinkers we know, independently of the notion of an obligation, what a promise is, and that it obliges is a logical accident, a fact dependent upon the manifest utility in the world in which we happen to live of the practice of promising and promise-keeping.

The rule-utilitarianism to which I shall now turn, the view once suggested by Rawls,[6] and since then widely echoed by others, is not so contemptuous of common sense. A promise obliges—this is self-evident—and so far traditional deontologists, it is conceded, have had uncommonly good sense on their side. The rule concerning promises, far from embodying mere empirical findings, is self-evident; but the self-evidence of the rule is derived from the fact that the rule defines the term "promise." Here the logical relation between promise and rule is reversed. On the older view the notion of a promise was thought to be intelligible independently of the rule. On the present view the rule is logically prior to the concept of a promise. It is not that, as in the case of a custom, or of what is done as a rule, or of that which one makes it a rule to do, we need first of all to understand the relevant act in order to understand the custom or the thing one does as a rule or the thing one makes it a rule to do. On the contrary, were it not for the promise-rule we should have no conception of what a promise is; for, by defining promises as acts by which obligations are created, the rule establishes or creates the required logical connection between promise and the obligatory feature of promise-keeping acts.

Here of course the model of a defining rule is a rule of a game. Rules of this kind serve to define the activity or practice that *is* the game by specifying offices, moves, privileges, etc., an understanding of which is necessary for the understanding of what the game is. On this analogy it would appear to be impossible to understand what a bishop is in a game of chess independently of the diagonal move specified by the

[6] "Two Concepts of Rules," *The Philosophical Review*, LXIV (1955).

bishop-rule. Just as the bishop-rule defines and thus identifies the bishop, so the promise-rule defines and thus identifies the promise. There is no bishop before, over and above, or independently of the bishop-rule; and there is no promising independently of the promise-rule and the obligation it establishes.

The present version of rule-utilitarianism is clearly distinct from that of either Hume or Mill. It is not desirable or useful, but logically imperative, that we refrain from citing utility in justification of any particular act. It would be a logical howler to suppose that utility *could* justify particular acts. It would be as preposterous to defend moving one's bishop diagonally on the ground that it made everyone happier. Why do such and such here and now either in the moral or the chess game? The rule and only the rule is relevant. Why adopt this rather than that rule? Here and only at this point does it even make sense to appeal to utility. There are, then, two distinct levels of justification to which radically different sorts of considerations apply.

The view is also different from that of Toulmin. On the present view the rule is relevant not because it refers us to the done thing—a custom or practice with its regular form of behavior to which we can adjust our own—but because, by defining the promise, it *establishes* the obligation as its built-in feature.

V

The view is not without merit. Those who propound it have made much, and rightly so, of the importance of the context of moral reasoning: the roles, offices and transactions of agents, in order to emphasize the conceptual connection between such practical affairs and the obligatory features of particular acts. But it is with the specific game analogy employed, the attempt to elucidate moral reasoning by using the model of a defining rule of a game, that I am now concerned. And I shall argue that this model will not work. Indeed, I shall argue that the connection between promise and the obligatoriness of the promise-keeping act is thereby much too tightly drawn even if, *per impossibile,* such rules could justify our doings. I shall argue that it is only by reference to that very context of moral reasoning that the obligation of promises and the rightness of promise-keeping acts can be elucidated, but in a manner that is obscured by the preoccupation with defining rules. Indeed I want to express grave doubts about any two-level program of justification: the restriction to particular acts of the appeal to rules and the restriction to rules of the appeal to utility.

VI

We are told that we are to justify particular acts only by means of the relevant rule. The rule is held to be an identifying rule of a practice, one that defines the act that falls under it in the way in which, for example, the bishop-rule, by defining "bishop-move" and "bishop," enable us to identify the bishop and the moves it makes. If, then, the rule that one ought to keep one's promises justifies the claim that a particular act is obligatory, it does so by defining promise-keeping as obligatory and by enabling us to identify the particular act as the promise-keeping act it is. The following considerations show that this will not do.

(a) Let us assume that the claim is true. Then there could no more be an exception to the promise-rule than there could be valid exceptions to the bishop-rule. An exception in the latter case would destroy the identity of the move as a possible move in the game of chess. So an exception to the former would destroy its identity as an act in the moral game. So-called exceptions, in morals as in chess, if permissible, must be built into the rules in the way in which the exceptional but unexceptionable first move of the pawn, two squares forward, is a permissible exception to the general run of pawn moves, but not to the pawn-rule itself. It is for this reason that we are explicitly asked to think of the so-called exceptions merely as more detailed specifications of what the rules actually state.[7] Since, however, moral rules also serve to justify particular acts, they are, so understood, as airtight as any directive can possibly be, informing us of what in any given situation we are duty-bound to do. Let us assume what seems patently false, namely, that every admissible so-called exception, can be foreseen and hence built into a rule that is now devoid of exceptions. Then moral reasoning degenerates, on this view, into the subsumption of particular cases under airtight general rules, and every moral dilemma so-called is simply an instance of a confused apprehension of what the relevant moral rule actually states.

(b) But the attempt to combine the justifying and the defining functions of rules cannot succeed. Consider the analogy: the rule that defines "bishop" and "bishop-move" does not require a player to make a move, and neither does it guide him in any move he does make. It gives him absolutely no reason for making any move. Someone who knows the game has no need to be informed or reminded of the bishop-rule. And if he wants to know whether moving this bishop in these circumstances is the right move to make, it is both irrelevant and impertinent to tell him "This is how the bishop is moved." At best the answer to the question "How does the bishop move?" can only prepare the ground for the further and distinct question with which those who know the game are concerned, namely, whether this or that move is wise, right or sound. So it is in the practical settings in which promises are made and usually kept. If the promise-rule *defines* "promise" and thereby establishes the obligation as the built-in feature of the promise, then at best it answers the conceptual or technical question "What is a promise?" and "How is it kept?" But as such it cannot answer the further question with which

[7] As Rawls (*loc. cit.*, 27) put it, ". . . a particular case cannot be an exception to a rule of a practice. An exception is rather a qualification or a further specification of the rule."

a responsible agent is concerned, of the wisdom in particular circumstances of offering a promise, or, having made one that he can now keep, of the rightness or soundness of doing so.

This result is not surprising. The supposition that moral rules are employed in the justification of particular acts implies that the acts to be justified are intelligible as the acts they are even when justifications are wanting. Alternatively, if moral rules are logically prior to the acts they define, then citing the rule is not providing a reason for the act so defined. One does not justify by defining, but only by citing warranting facts. An appeal to a practice, like Wittgenstein's appeal to the language-game, may elucidate a concept, but it does not and cannot demonstrate the truth of a claim, least of all the one that here and now this or that specific act is obligatory.

(c) There is, admittedly, a conceptual connection between the promise and the obligatoriness of the promise-keeping act. For the fact that, for example, in giving someone a sum of money, one is keeping a promise is *as such* a good reason for doing so. And if there is no other relevant consideration that bears upon that act, it follows logically that one ought to do it. So, too, there is a conceptual connection between punishment and guilt. But the latter connection does not warrant the preposterous claim that only the guilty ought to be punished on the ground that punishment would not be punishment, but mere hurt or injury if, willfully, it were meted out to the innocent. And the former cannot justify the equally specious contention that one ought to keep this or that promise on the ground that promises would not be promises if we failed to keep them. For the promise-rule does not define or establish the connection between promise and obligatory act in the way in which the bishop-rule defines or establishes the relation between bishop and bishop-move. But it is logically impossible—and this is secured by the bishop-rule—that the bishop should move straight across the board in the way the castle does. Failure during chess play to move a piece diagonally by moving it in some other way, this being a legally permissible move, *establishes* that it is not the bishop but some other piece that is being moved. But failure to restrict punishment to the guilty does not establish that it is not really punishment. Neither does failure to keep one's solemn word establish that one has not promised. Failure *vis à vis* the bishop-rule exempts one from the criticism that one has made the wrong or unwise move, however much it may expose one to other criticisms (e.g., that one has cheated or that one does not know the game at all). But failure in respect to promises carries with it no corresponding exemption.

If there is a conceptual connection between promise and obligatory act, it is not the tight connection established by something like a defining rule of a game.

(d) Let us here ignore the deviant and the parasitic cases of promises to do the immoral or the impossible, and confine our attention to the central cases by reference to which we do come to understand what a promise is, for it is to such cases that the promise-rule has primary application.

To begin with, the rule that one ought to keep one's promises no more defines "promise" than the rule that one ought to tell the truth defines truth-telling. In the case of bishop and bishop-move the bishop-rule is necessary and sufficient. No doubt there is a conceptual connection between a promise and the obligatoriness of the promise-keeping act—that was recognized long before rule-utilitarianism came into vogue—but the connection is not established by means of a definition or a defining rule. There are other ways of exhibiting connections of ideas. And, in the case of the promise, what has been obscured by the preoccupation with defining rules of games is the importance of the moral context within which alone "I promise . . ." is intelligible as the promise locution it is, and, within which, too, a relation between persons is established by the promise, namely, an obligation *to the person* to whom the promise is given and, correlatively, the right of the promisee with respect to the promiser.

It is this obligation *to a person* that needs to be distinguished from, conceptually related, as indeed it is, to the obligatory feature *of an act* by which the obligation is honored and met. The fact that one is under an obligation that one can meet is a good reason (but perhaps not a sufficient one) for performing the obligation-meeting act. And supposing that there are no other relevant circumstances, it follows that one ought to perform that act. It would be logically incoherent to concede one's obligation, one's ability and opportunity then and there to meet it, and the absence of any other relevant consideration, but deny that one ought to do the promise-keeping deed. The fact that there is a conceptual or logical relation between these two concepts, both marked by the word "obligation" is precisely what one would expect given our sense that the promise, implying as it does the establishment of a new relation between the persons involved, is *as such* a good reason for performing the promise-keeping act.

But how shall we elucidate this notion of an obligation between persons, if not by means of a defining rule? Surely the answer lies in the actual method commonly employed by us in the moral instruction we give the young. To explain this relation we need only exhibit the manner in which the obligation can be met, including the ways in which one may be released from one's obligation by the word and will of those to whom one is bound, by their waiving or forfeiting their rights in the matter. Further, it is an essential feature of such instruction that attention is directed to the manner in which a variety of competing considerations may be weighed and, in this or that set of circumstances, may outweigh the obligation created by the promise; that attention is also directed to the various liabilities incurred by one's poor judgment in such matters and by one's thoughtless oversights and deliberate omissions and failures, and to the manner, depending upon our relations with the party and our good estimate of his sensibilities, in which the previously existing relation of mutual trust and respect may perhaps be restored. It is this and even more—depending upon the special circumstances of the case, certainly no mere defining rule of a practice patterned after any rule of any game, but a whole way of thinking *and* feeling *and* doing—that is involved in the understanding we gain, through our moral training and instruction, of the nature of the obligation created by the promise and the manner in which that obligation is decisive in establishing as obligatory a given promise-keeping act.

In short, it is in the lives as lived by responsible and considerate persons that the relation between persons established by promises is to be elucidated, not by means of a defining rule of a practice and not by the tautology that a promise obliges, that is, that a promise creates an obligation.

(e) Rule-utilitarians who have employed the analogy of a defining rule of a game and who have been led on that account to a two-level theory of justification according to which it would be absurd in principle to attempt to justify particular acts in terms of utility, are surely in error. On this point any game analogy would appear to collapse. Consider tactical and strategic rules of play. It is good tactics to move one's knights and bishops into play early in the game and it is good strategy to command the center of the board. These are some of the rules or principles which do guide players —not the defining rules with which rule-utilitarians have been preoccupied. But while these rules serve to justify, they may not be employed mechanically without proper attention to circumstances; for in special cases it would be poor playing indeed to be bound by them. In these respects they provide better points of analogy with our ordinary moral rules than do the defining rules of the game. Yet this analogy too may mislead. For it would be as absurd to argue for the tactical and strategic moves specified by these rules on the ground that they would make everyone concerned happier as it does for the diagonal move specified by the bishop-rule. Tactical and strategic rules are adopted because they improve one's chances of winning, not because they maximize our pleasures or satisfactions. But promising is an eminently useful device. And we do sometimes justify breaking a promise on the ground of utility. In short, in all of these game analogies it is logically impermissible to cite utility in justification of particular moves; but in our practical affairs utility can and does serve to justify our doings.

The fact that such justifications are open to us is by no means surprising. Not all practical reasons are moral reasons, and life would be arid indeed if we were largely preoccupied with them. Utility, while not as such perhaps a *moral* reason, is surely one of the considerations to which reasonable persons attend. If, rightly, I go to the theatre instead of staring all evening at the television, am I thereby committed to the view that I am duty-bound to amuse myself? And it is not an excessively rare case in which one is reasonable and justified by utility, in refusing to keep a promise that is in itself trifling or no longer of any concern to the promisee. But where in such cases utility does justify, it may not do so at the expense of that mutual respect and confidence that marks our relations to the persons concerned. It is this that the non-performance of promises may jeopardize and that explanations, excuses and apologies are designed to safeguard and, if need be, to restore. Certainly, one who has received a promise would be unreasonable, if, recognizing the inutility of the promise-keeping act, he demanded his rights on the ground that promises are promises and sacrosanct.

VII

It is a truism that pleasure is good. But this hardly warrants that classic case of neglect of context, the view that anything worth having for its own sake would be good if it existed, as G. E. Moore once put it "in absolute isolation," as a sort of wholly isolated blob of intrinsic goodness.[8] For the goods we prize are the goods that human beings, of the sort that you and I are, find and achieve in the kinds of lives

---

[8] *Principia Ethica* (Cambridge, 1903), p. 187.

we live. The fact that something is pleasant is *as such* a good reason for wanting and getting it, but surely not *no matter what* the circumstances may be. For that only leads to the familiar bit of philosophical nonsense that an act of cruelty in which one took delight would, so far at least and in itself, be all the better for the pleasure it gave the agent. Utility is a good reason for this or that action, but only within the context in which the moral proprieties are observed.

It is this neglect of the moral context that emerges in the utilitarian's two-level account of justification. It is of course plainly false to think of morality as constituted or defined by a system of rules. That would present us as a model for moral reasoning the rule-bound thinking of a moral tyro who is helpless whenever confronted, not merely by the rare and difficult moral dilemmas seldom cited as examples of moral problems in ethics textbooks, and which few of us, fortunately, are called upon to resolve, but by the not infrequent and easily disposable cases involving competing rules. Even in games like chess it would be absurd to think of reasoning as the simple-minded subsumption of particular cases under rules or principles. For there are exceptional cases in which one could be fully justified in relinquishing control of the center of the board notwithstanding the rule. And the promise-rule does not state that regardless of circumstances one is duty-bound in every particular situation in which one finds oneself to keep one's promise, given of course that this can be done. A promise obliges—this, surely, follows from the very meaning of the word—and the force of the rule, that one ought to keep one's promises, is to remind us of a consideration which, normally, is decisive. But the *onus probandi* is always on the promiser, and it is this that cannot be settled by definitions but only by the facts: whether the situation is a normal one or, given that there are other relevant considerations, whether these do or do not warrant departing from the general rule. Neither in chess nor in our daily lives is wisdom or good judgment a matter of blindly following the rules. Nor will it do to argue that, since there are no air-tight rules that relieve us of the necessity of using our good judgment, the difference between wisdom and witlessness is all a matter of sentiment or a sheer unreasoned decision or volition. What is required of us is no mere subsumption of particular cases under rules, but a nice judgment of how best to serve the interests of all those affected by what we do including *always* just that interest we have in maintaining mutual trust and respect. We must decide not simply on the basis of utility when we must choose between competing moral rules or principles, but how in those circumstances to serve utility while maintaining proper moral relations with all those affected by our conduct.

For our choice in morals, unlike that in chess or in any institution or social arrangement defined by a set of rules, is not whether or not to play the moral game, but whether to play it well or badly. One can decide whether or not to prom-ise, to speak, to assume this or that obligation; and one can choose between doing and not doing one's duty. But what would it be like to withdraw from morality itself as one can from a game, political party or social club? In the latter cases one remains a human being. But suppose one sloughs off, not only the obligations that go with one's office, job, role in a game, political organization or other social arrangement, but also the obligations one has to one's parents or children or spouse, and even those elementary obligations we have to human beings, thereby losing any concern for anyone else as a being to whom any consideration of any kind is due in word, thought or deed. The supposition does more than tax the imagination; it asks us to think of others not as the hu-man beings they are and with whom, only as human beings, we can have dealings of any kind, in games, institutions or in any of our casual transactions. For no such affair can take place in a moral vacuum, any more than can the transaction of giving and receiving promises. These are affairs into which only human beings like ourselves can enter, persons who, in

Locke's words, are concerned and accountable. In short, the institutions and games and other practices defined by rules presuppose for their occurrence the very moral status of persons which the analogy with such arrangements is designed by rule-utilitarians to elucidate.

And this brings me to my final comments on the place of utility in ethics. In their talk of justifying morality, rule-utilitarians have supposed that morality is to be justified by its consequential utility, a utility which lies beyond morality itself since it is produced by morality and hence a utility that is intelligible as a good reason independently of the morality that is its source. Now what it would mean to justify morality itself, a matter about which we have no choice at all, is surely unclear. We can indeed justify an institution, for it is up to us to join it or not, to establish it or to withdraw from it. And we can justify those doings in which we do well as moral agents. Here we do have a choice. But it makes no sense to speak of justifying morality itself, for here we have no choice at all. Further, consider the alleged justification of the so-called "institution of morality" in terms of utility, as if utility in itself, and quite independently of the morality that is its alleged source, could provide such a reason. For utility is a good reason, I have argued, only within the context in which the relevant moralities are honored in thought and deed, and in which moral self-respect is maintained. The proper attention paid to what is due to persons is the minimum background presupposed in a legitimate appeal to utility as a justifying consideration. And the good to be achieved by reasonable human action is not a consequence of our moral practice—something in which morality itself eventuates and which thus lies beyond morality. It is rather the good to be achieved wholly within the framework of morality itself.

Utility does indeed have a place in our practical reasoning, but only against an existing moral background, which, being background, is all too easily lost to view. And what utilitarians have done, in assimilating morality with institutions, and the justification of the former with that of the latter, is thus implicitly to presuppose the very moral matters to be explained and the moral context within which any justification of any sort is possible.

ETHICAL FALLIBILITY

Charles L. Stevenson

CHARLES L. STEVENSON, Professor of Philosophy at the University of Michigan, has also taught at Yale University and at Harvard University. He was a Guggenheim fellow (1945–46) and served as President of the Western Division of the American Philosophical Association (1961–62). He has published articles on ethics and aesthetics both in the United States and abroad. He is the author of *Ethics and Language* (1944) and *Facts and Values* (1963).

INTRODUCTION

My purpose, in this paper, will be to develop one step further a conception of ethics that I worked out some years ago; so I must begin by giving you a brief summary of what that conception is. In particular, I must explain how I distinguish between normative ethics and the sciences. That will take up the first section of my paper, where I must beg the indulgence of those of you who have previously become familiar with my work. In the remaining three sections I shall go on to my principal topic, namely, ethical fallibility, hoping to show that my conception of ethics can provide an intelligible place for it.

Charles L. Stevenson

I. SOME COMPARISONS BETWEEN SCIENCE
AND ETHICS

An important difference between science and ethics, in my opinion, is found in their disparate uses of *language*. The situation is roughly this: a scientific sentence typically expresses the speaker's belief, and invites others to share that belief; whereas an ethical sentence, though in many ways connected with beliefs, typically expresses the speaker's attitude and invites others to share that attitude. But let me explain further.

There can be little doubt that a scientific sentence typically expresses the speaker's belief—or if you will, the speaker's or writer's belief at the time that he speaks or writes, the possibility of lies being allowed for. It need not, of course, express a belief that is peculiar to the speaker, who may have inherited it from a long scientific tradition; and it need not, in view of the difficulties of scientific inquiry, express a true belief. But it remains the case that it typically expresses a belief. When I add that a scientific sentence typically *invites* others to share the speaker's belief, I am of course using a figure of speech; for "invites" is in some cases too polite a term, and is likely to suggest, quite wrongly, that those whom the speaker is addressing can believe or disbelieve at will. But I trust that my meaning is clear: having expressed a belief, the speaker expects the hearers either to accept it or else to explain why they cannot accept it.

Now with regard to beliefs I want to *contrast* scientific sentences with ethical sentences, but I do not, of course, want to say that the latter have nothing to do with beliefs. When we say that a judge has made a *just* decision we are usually guided by many beliefs, including, for instance, the belief that the judge did not accept a bribe. To be sure, ethical sentences introduce beliefs more ambiguously than scientific sentences do—and indeed, "ambiguously" is perhaps too weak a term in this connection. But ethical sentences manifestly "suggest" beliefs, or as Nowell-Smith puts it, they contextually imply them.

The point that I want to emphasize, then, is concerned not with the absence of beliefs, but rather with the presence of attitudes, in ethics. By "attitudes" I refer to tendencies to be for or against something, as typified by liking, disliking, approving, disapproving, favoring, disfavoring, and so on. Now it is not the function of scientific sentences, in their expression of beliefs, to go on to express the speaker's attitude to something, or to invite others to share that attitude. But ethical sentences, in my opinion, typically *do* go on to express the speaker's attitude, and they typically *do* go on to invite others to share that attitude.

Why do I say that ethical sentences "express" the speaker's attitude, as distinct, for instance, from saying that they "describe" the speaker's attitude? The reason becomes apparent when we think back to the situation I have just mentioned in connection with science. An astronomer, in speaking about the heavens, is expressing his beliefs but is clearly not describing his beliefs. To say the latter would imply that he was engaged in introspective psychology, and not in astronomy. In the same way, I want to suggest, a man who says, for instance, that democracy is a good form of government, is expressing his attitude to democracy, and is not describing his attitude to it. If he were merely describing it he too would be engaged in introspective psychology; and whatever else ethics may be, it is clearly not introspective psychology. So we have this parallel, along with an important difference: just as an astronomer cannot tell us about the heavens without expressing his beliefs, so a writer on normative ethics cannot tell us about the value of democracy without expressing his attitudes; but neither man is merely talking about himself.

Somewhat similarly, I say that an ethical sentence typically "invites" the attitude of others, as distinct from saying that it "describes" their attitudes. When a man says that democracy is a good form of government he is not simply describing some favorable attitude to democracy that is prevalent, say, in his community. The favorable attitude may in fact be prevalent; but in calling democracy "good" he is normally trying to strengthen and preserve that favorable attitude, not just to take note of the fact that it exists. And if the favorable attitude is not prevalent, then he is normally trying to make it *become* prevalent.

We have, then, a marked difference between the function of scientific sentences and the function of ethical sentences. Much more could be said about this difference, but I must now leave it, and turn, in order, to three further topics—the topics of *uncertainty, disagreement,* and *reasons.*

An element of uncertainty, and often rather more than an "element" of it, may arise in either science or ethics; but the uncertainty is not of the same sort. In science it is a hesitation between belief and disbelief, and may accordingly be called uncertainty *in belief.* In ethics it is usually that in part, and in good part, but for the rest is something else, which may appropriately be called uncertainty *in attitude.* It usually takes the form of conflicting attitudes, as in cases where we are inclined to be *for* something and at the same time to be *against* it. A voter, for instance, may find that he approves of a certain party's policy on national affairs but disapproves of its policy on international affairs; so he may be uncertain whether or not he ought to vote for the party. His uncertainty, which is in attitude, may be largely *due to* his uncertainty in belief about the details and long-range results of the party's policies; but that, of course, is not to say that the one sort of uncertainty can be identified with the other.

We now have a second difference between science and ethics. Just as the sentences of science typically express and invite beliefs, whereas those of ethics typically go on to express and invite attitudes, so the uncertainty in science is in belief, whereas that in ethics is (in part) in attitude.

What I have said about uncertainty can very nearly be repeated with regard to disagreement. Uncertainty may involve only one individual, whereas disagreement involves more than one, but both are alike in being prods to problem solving. Now the disagreements that we have in science are *in belief*—which is only to say that one person or group is inclined to believe something that another person or group is inclined to disbelieve, and that they argue on that account. But in ethics, once again, we have something more; for an important kind of disagreement that there arises is a disagreement *in attitude*. One group approves of segregated schools, for example, and the other group disapproves of them; so they argue on *that* account.

It is important, in this connection, to note the following very simple point: in ethics disagreement can give place to agreement only if someone's attitude changes, whereas in science that is not the case.

My remarks are pointing in the direction of a generalization: having described science we can go on to describe ethics by replacing or supplementing the term "belief" by the term "attitude." Though very rough, the generalization is perhaps not too rough to be instructive. Let me now illustrate it further with regard to *reasons*—that being the most important of these introductory topics, the others serving mainly to prepare the way for it.

It will be obvious, both in science and in ethics, that we can attempt to give reasons for what we say. But proceeding in the same manner as before I want to distinguish reasons of two sorts.

Since a scientist's language, as we have seen, typically expresses his beliefs and invites others to share them, his reasons in support of what he says are an attempt to give a certain backing to these beliefs. And when he considers reasons that seem to count against what he says, he is wondering whether his beliefs should not, perhaps, give place to disbeliefs. The reasons can accordingly be called reasons for believing or disbelieving. But in ethics we have a different situation. To the extent that a speaker's sentences express his attitudes, and invite others to share them, he needs reasons that will give a certain backing to his *attitudes*. And any reasons that seem to count against his judgment will lead him to wonder whether or not to alter or redirect his attitudes. So the characteristic reasons are no longer reasons for believing or disbelieving but instead are reasons for approving or disapproving—or more generally, reasons for favoring or disfavoring.

The latter reasons require further examination. Considered in themselves they are usually statements of the sort found in the sciences, or in the common-sense counterparts of the sciences. They are selected and organized, however, in a manner intended to guide the attitudes that a given ethical problem may involve, and they become relevant to ethics on that account. They can guide attitudes, moreover, in a way that Hume, among others, saw with some little clarity. When a man begins by approving of X, his attitude to it may change as he acquires or calls to mind various beliefs about X's nature and consequences; for these may reveal objects of his other attitudes, and the force of these other attitudes may then become transferred to X, either strengthening the man's favor of it, or weakening it, or transforming it into disfavor.

Since the reasons in question are selected to guide attitudes, and since attitudes can be variously guided, we cannot expect the reasons that support or attack an ethical judgment to fall within any *one* special science. In deciding whether we ought to redouble our efforts to avoid another world war, for instance, the reasons that bear on our conclusions will some of them deal with the economic consequences of war; but there will be others that bear on the psychological, sociological, and political consequences of war; and there will be still others, in our atomic age, that bear on its physical and chemical consequences, and on its biological consequences. The reasons that become relevant to an ethical issue, then, are no less varied than they are numerous; and that, in the main, is why we find ethical questions so hard to answer.

II. FALLIBILITY IN SCIENCE AND IN ETHICS

Having now summarized my general conception of ethics I can go on to my main topic. As my title suggests, I shall discuss our willingness, throughout much of our everyday life, to acknowledge our *fallibility* in ethics—or in other words, our willingness to acknowledge that our judgments must often be held open to correction, as distinct from being proclaimed in a manner implying that we have said the last word. Does my conception of ethics, I want to ask, provide a proper place for fallibility, and can it help to clarify the *sort* of fallibility that arises?

It will be convenient to follow the same procedure that I followed above—that of beginning with simple observations about the sciences, and of seeing to what extent they suggest parallel observations about ethics. So with a promise of returning to ethics in just a moment, let me first call attention to some of the ways in which we might affirm or deny our scientific fallibility.

It will be evident that the remark, "Everything that I believe to be the case actually is the case," would proclaim the speaker's *in*fallibility with regard to his scientific conclusions (and indeed, even with regard to factual conclusions too trivial to be included with science). And none of us, of course, would seriously make such a remark. We do not let our vanity get the better of us to quite that extent.

At the other extreme, the remark, "Everything that I believe to be the case actually is not the case," would indicate that the speaker is invariably in error, and would again not be made seriously. The statement has even its near-logical peculiarities; for if a speaker should affirm an instance of it, saying, "I believe, for example, that hydrogen is an element, but it isn't," his remark would be of the kind commonly classified as a "self-defeating" one, or as a "pragmatic contradiction."

We have a quite different remark, however, in "Many things that I believe to be the case *may* not be the case." This permits the speaker to acknowledge his fallibility (which must be contrasted both with an infallibility and an invariable incorrectness), and is entirely congenial to science and to common sense.

We have a variant of this third remark, and under circumstances that are presumably appropriate, in such an example as this. A schoolboy asks his teacher whether there is any animal life on Mars. The teacher replies, "According to me there isn't; but you must remember that what I believe on such a matter may not be the case." Here the teacher is careful to acknowledge his fallibility, rather than take it for granted; for the boy may naïvely suppose that his teacher, if not infallible, is very nearly so.

Acknowledgments of fallibility are not always appropriate, to be sure, and on occasion may be altogether artificial. Suppose, for example, that our schoolboy had asked whether the Allegheny Mountains were in America. The teacher would then, presumably, have been content just to tell him. Any addition of "Or so I believe, but of course they may not be," would indicate that the teacher was seriously ignorant of geography—or alternatively, perhaps, that the teacher had read too much of Russell and too little of Moore.

But however that may be, I think you will agree that the occasions on which we allow for the possibility of our errors, appropriately saying that what we believe to be the case may not be the case, are decidedly numerous. We acknowledge our fallibility in this fashion not, usually, because we hesitate to live by such beliefs as we have, but only because we feel that on an intellectual journey, as the well-known quotation puts it, it is better to travel than to arrive, traveling being a kind of constant arriving.

But what shall be said of ethics? How, in that discipline, do we protest our fallibility? And to what extent is it possible, once again, to contrast ethics with science by emphasizing attitudes rather than beliefs?

To answer, let me suggest an ethical parallel to the *in*-fallibility-protesting remark, "Everything that I believe to be the case actually is the case." Perhaps the closest parallel is this: "Everything that my attitudes, guided by the beliefs that attend them, lead me to consider good, bad, right, wrong, obligatory, and so on, is something that really is good, bad, right, wrong, obligatory, and so on." But for simplicity I shall abridge this to "Everything that meets with my approval is right."

For the purposes of comparison, then, we have the remarks, "Everything that I believe to be the case actually is the case," and "Everything that meets with my approval is right." And there can be little doubt that the remarks are similar—similar, of course, in their absurdity. Just as the one indicates that the speaker is not preparing to reconsider any of his beliefs, so the other indicates that he is not preparing to reconsider any of his attitudes. And just as the one gives us little hope for a two-way discussion with him on science, so the other gives us little hope for a two-way discussion with him on ethics—for he will think that he can gain nothing from what we say, and will expect us, so long as he abides by his remark, to listen to him as his disciples. So as *we* are likely to see the speaker, though not as he sees himself, he is in either case a man who has become fixated at his present stage of mental development.

For purposes of terminological symmetry, then, I propose to say that the first remark would protest the speaker's infallibility in belief and that the second would protest his infallibility in attitude—using "in belief" and "in attitude" just as I did in connection with uncertainty and disagreement. But I must make this further point: Instead of using the deliberately over-simplified example, "Everything that meets with my approval is right," I might alternatively have used the slightly more complicated example, "Everything that my approval, guided by such beliefs as may attend it, leads me to consider right *is* right." This latter example, by mentioning beliefs, helps to show that a protestation of ethical infallibility would be concerned with beliefs and attitudes together. For here as elsewhere the distinguishing feature of ethics is found not in the absence of beliefs but in the special presence of attitudes.

Let me now suggest an ethical parallel to the other absurd remark that I mentioned above—the one that ran, "Everything that I believe to be the case is actually not the case." We have such a parallel in "Everything that meets with my approval is wrong." And again we have a muddleheadedness. In illustrating the remark the speaker will say such curious things as, "I approve of segregation, and it is wrong," "I approve of socialized medicine, and it is wrong," and so on. The muddleheadedness arises whenever he is not using "wrong" as a short way of saying "considered wrong by others." We then want to ask, "But if you really approve of it, what's the point of saying that it's wrong?" And we would be likely to use the same indignant tone of voice that we would use, for the parallel example from science, in asking, "But if you really believe that it's the case, what's the point of saying that it isn't?"

These absurdities are of interest, of course, only because they help us to understand an ordinary acknowledgment of ethical *falli*bility. Now just as scientific fallibility, as we have seen, can be acknowledged by the remark, "Many things that I believe to be the case may not be the case," so ethical fallibility can be acknowledged by the remark, "Many things that meet with my approval may not be right." In comparing these remarks I need only review in reverse, so to speak, what I have previously said with regard to infallibility; but let me spell out the comparison even so:

In the first place, the remark, "Many things that I believe to be the case may not be the case," acknowledges a fallibility in belief, whereas the remark, "Many things that meet with my approval may not be right," acknowledges in the first instance a fallibility in attitude—though it implicitly acknowledges, as well, a fallibility in belief to whatever extent the speaker's attitudes are guided by beliefs.

In the second place, an acknowledgment of ethical fallibility, no less than an acknowledgment of scientific fallibility, indicates that the speaker is prepared, on further reflection, to change his mind. And that will be encouraging to the rest of us. We can hope for a two-way discussion with him, and need not fear that we shall be expected to listen to him as his disciples.

In the third place, an acknowledgment of fallibility in ethics, as in science, is usually of a restricted sort, rather than of a perfectly general sort. Just as the teacher in my earlier example acknowledged fallibility with regard to animal life on Mars but not with regard to the location of the Allegheny Mountains, so he might acknowledge fallibility with regard to the rightness or wrongness of capital punishment, say, but not with regard to the rightness or wrongness of cruelty for its own sake.

In the fourth place, and finally, we can have in ethics, as well as in science, a conception of travel as a kind of constant arriving. A man who is willing to reconsider his ethical judgments, and to welcome discussions and inquiries that may lead him to do so, does not thereby become half-hearted in his attitudes, or hesitant to live by them and to defend them. The reasons that now guide his attitudes, and give them strength by causing them to work together, are no less a source of confidence than those further reasons that may redirect and alter his attitudes later on; so he does not have to postpone taking a stand on an ethical issue until that ever-receding date on which *all* reasons for approving or disapproving are known to him.

III. THE MODUS OPERANDI OF REMARKS THAT ACKNOWLEDGE FALLIBILITY

I am not, of course, simply pointing out that a great many people actually acknowledge their fallibility in ethics. That I take for granted. I am trying to show, rather, that my general conception of ethics can readily find a place for fallibility, and can help to explain its nature. And for this purpose I must carry my analysis a step or two further. Let me now do so, with a more careful attention to the typical functions of scientific and ethical language.

Consider once more, then, the infallibility-protesting remark, oriented to the sciences, that runs, "Everything that I believe to be the case actually is the case." The first part of this remark, with its overt use of the word "believe," is evidently *about*, and thus is making a *reference to*, the speaker's beliefs; and in making this reference to them the speaker is not yet expressing them or inviting others to share them. He is simply mentioning beliefs that belong to a certain class, namely the class of them that are his. But when he continues his sentence, saying that everything that he believes to be the case "actually is the case," he is not making any additional reference to his beliefs. Rather, he is implicitly expressing all of the beliefs that he previously referred to, and is inviting others to share them.

I use the qualifying word, "implicitly," for an obvious reason. The speaker is not, by his generalization, enumerating his beliefs one by one and thereafter expressing them one by one, or inviting others to share them one by one. But if he were exhaustively illustrating his generalization he would have to give us such an enumeration. Thus he might begin by saying, "I believe that the air contains neon," so far only referring to his belief; and he would add, "and the air *does* contain neon," thereby expressing that belief and inviting others to share it. Similarly, he might continue, "I believe that hydrogen is an element," so far only referring to his belief; and he would add, "and hydrogen *is* an element," thereby expressing that belief and inviting others to share it. And so on. So in an intelligible sense his infallibility-protesting generalization, having referred to all his beliefs, goes on "implicitly" to express them all, and to invite others to share them all.

Now why is the speaker absurd? Why do we immediately

suspect him of being fixated, as I have put it, at his present state of development? The answer is evident when we consider the *blanket way* in which he has proceeded. If he had been content to mention just *one* of his beliefs, and had proceeded to express it alone, all would have been well. He is surely privileged to express any manageable-sized belief that he has; for we can then, and perhaps profitably, discuss it with him, and decide on the basis of our own reflections whether or not to agree. But when he implicitly expresses all of his beliefs, and invites us to accept them all—even before we know what they will turn out to be—the prospect of a profitable discussion with him on this multitude of disconnected and yet-to-be discovered topics simply vanishes.

This is particularly evident in connection with the *invitation* that attends his remark. We can accept the invitation if we are content to be his disciples, and thus see no need for discussion; but otherwise we can only raise our eyebrows, since the invitation is such a blanket one that it doesn't assist us in locating a topic on which a two-way discussion is likely to arise.

But the same is true with regard to the *expressing* function (as distinct from the inviting function) of his infallibility-protesting remark. For the various beliefs that he has will include some, no doubt, that he might be expected to hold with rather less than full conviction. But in fact he is expressing them all. And why should he be so anxious to express them unless he is attempting to give them a more secure place in his thinking, *preventing* any from being held with less than a full conviction? In effect, then, he is reviewing all his beliefs, and is expressing them all in a manner that will tend to immunize him from any considerations that would otherwise lead him to revise or change them. And with this there comes a lack of incentive on his part to participate in any further inquiry, or any discussion of a two-way sort. His expression of any one, manageably-sized belief, of course, would involve quite another situation; for a person who refuses to establish *any* belief more securely in his habits of thinking will end by being sieve-minded rather than open-minded. But a person who establishes all of his beliefs in this manner, and all of them at once, is clearly headed toward that intellectual fixation with which a protestation of infallibility is so closely allied.

These observations are readily transferred, *mutatis mutandis*, to ethics. If we return to the remark, "Everything that meets with my approval is right," we can readily see that this protestation of ethical infallibility begins by talking about, and thus by referring to, the speaker's attitudes. And it then goes on to *express* all these attitudes (by means of the word "right") and to invite us to share them. It expresses and invites attitudes "implicitly," of course; but it does indeed do that. How could we agree with the speaker without being prepared to take each and every one of his attitudes as our own?

Now the absurdity of the remark is evident, as before, simply because it expresses and invites in a blanket manner, and thus discourages discussion and inquiry. By his blanket *invitation* to us to share all his attitudes, the speaker requests so much that only his disciples could take him seriously, the rest of us being unable even to use his remark as a starting point for discussion. And by his blanket *expression* of his attitudes, he is taking steps, pretty clearly, to guard all of them from reconsideration. He is thus cutting himself off from any incentive to take part in discussions or to make inquiries that may lead his attitudes to change—the discussions and inquiries, of course. being potentially of a sort that might supply him with further reasons, including reasons for *dis*approving of what he now approves of.

It would be quite another thing (and note how close the parallel continues to be) if he expressed some one individual attitude, inviting us to share *that;* for he would then introduce an issue of manageable size, on which we might ask him for his reasons and give further reasons or counter-reasons in our turn. The issue would then permit a two-way discussion. But the speaker's blanket procedure, here no less than in the scientific case, is absurd because it tends to close all issues, rather than to keep them open to the correction of further thought and experience.

Thus our inclination to reject claims of infallibility in ethics, and our consequent respect for acknowledgments of fallibility, can easily be explained, and explained in a manner that connects them with corresponding aspects of science. The task of developing attitudes is no less complex than that of developing beliefs; and in neither case do most of us feel secure in affirming that the task has been completed once and for all. In this regard my general conception of ethics says nothing from which our common sense might be expected to recoil; and indeed, it does much to provide our common sense with an armor.

IV. FACTS AND VALUES THAT ARE "OUT THERE"

My discussion of fallibility has so far borne out the principle that I stated earlier in the paper: we can often say over again about ethics what we want to say about science, but with the proviso that we must replace or supplement the word "belief" by the word "attitude." In connection with fallibility, however, it may seem that the proviso becomes more than usually important—that it not only outweighs the parallels that I have mentioned, but outweighs them in a discouraging way. It may seem that a shift from beliefs to attitudes takes away our *incentive* for acknowledging fallibility, and thus makes any such acknowledgment in ethics, as compared with science, simply arbitrary. In the remainder of my paper, then, I want to consider whether that is so.

We acknowledge our fallibility in science, it may be urged, because we are convinced that the universe, as studied by science, is in some sense "out there" to be described. It is "out there" with all its facts, and the facts are not only the specific ones of geology, paleontology, history, and so on, but also the general ones that constitute the laws of nature. When we express beliefs about these facts, then, we are very far from being non-objective painters, who are free to make such designs as they will. Instead, we are realistic painters, intent on being faithful to what we are representing. Now it is our attempt to be faithful to the facts of the universe, it may be urged, that leads us to acknowledge our *scientific* fallibility. The facts may belie our beliefs, just as the objects that a realistic painter is painting may belie his picture. And that is why our acknowledgment of fallibility in science is in no way arbitrary. We have only to realize that our beliefs may depict the universe with faulty lines, so to speak, or faulty colors.

But in *ethics*, the objection continues, so long as that discipline is conceived as involving an expression of attitudes, we have no such situation. We of necessity become non-objective painters rather than realistic painters, for we find nothing "out there" for our attitudes to represent. There is normally, of course, some object or situation to which our attitudes are directed—something of whose nature our *beliefs*, guiding our attitudes, may or may not give us a faithful likeness; but our attitudes, as distinct from our beliefs about their objects, have nothing to do with representing anything. We are accordingly forced to say, with Russell, that "it is we who create value. . . . In this realm we are kings, and we debase our kingship if we bow down to nature." And why, it may be asked, so long as we accept *this* conception of ethics, should we have any incentive to acknowledge our fallibility? When we no longer have to fear that our judgments are unfaithful to something "out there," it may be urged, why should we evince anything more than a half-hearted willingness to revise them? Or alternatively (and the alternative is equally distressing) why should we not revise them capriciously, changing our judgments with each passing whim?

I am not, of course, quoting an objection that this or that philosopher has expressly formulated; but I do think that I am locating a genuine source of philosophical disquietude. It is the demand for something "out there" for our ethical judgments to copy, I suspect, that has led many theorists to reject an emphasis on attitudes in ethics, and to seek some other emphasis in its place.

Now in my opinion this demand is doubly mistaken: it is mistaken not only with regard to what it expects for ethics but also with regard to what it thinks it *has* for science. For in comparing a belief to a realistic painting the objection is naïve. It is naïve in a way that has repeatedly been pointed out in the theory of knowledge; but in ethics that tends to be forgotten and needs to be pointed out anew.

Let us remember, then, that a realistic painter has both his painting and his model in full view. So when he wants to correct his painting, in the interest of ensuring fidelity to his model, he can readily look from one to the other. He can "see" the one in the same sense that he can "see" the other. But what shall be said of the mental picture, so called, that a scientist paints of the facts—such facts, say, as those attending the origin of our planetary system. His mental picture, so called, may be a belief that the planets were torn from the sun by another sun that passed by. And if we want to become a little less tentative about this belief, making sure that it is faithful to the facts, it will be obvious that he does nothing similar to looking first at the origin of the planetary system and then at his beliefs. What he does, rather, is to accumulate as many reasons as he can that bear on the question. These reasons express further beliefs, which he adds to his whole body of beliefs. And although his whole body of beliefs meshes with experience at the edges, as Quine puts it, it remains the case that the meshing, being literally momentary, is not the same as model-copying.

It should be particularly noted that no *one* experience is sufficient to lead a scientist to change his belief; it is always some experience plus what he *brings to* that experience. And if it is urged that a *series* of experiences can be sufficient to make him change his belief, the answer is very simple. The earlier experiences in the series affect his belief only insofar as they are remembered; and his memories of them are themselves beliefs. That is to say, to remember is to believe in a certain way. The memories are not part of the so-called model, but are parts of the so-called picture.

So if we want to compare a belief to a painting at all—and I do not recommend this—we should make the comparison differently. We should compare it to a portrait that is considered suitable or unsuitable depending on whether or not it *goes* well with all the other portraits in the family gallery. That is to say, instead of supposing that the facts attending the origin of the planets help a scientist to check his beliefs about them, we can more appropriately say that the place of his beliefs about them in a system of beliefs permits him to check whether various alleged facts about the planets are really facts. Or to put it in more traditional terms, no insistence on facts will permit a man to avoid a coherence *test* of his beliefs; and it is the coherence that guides him in deciding which of his beliefs correspond to fact and which do not.

Let me now connect this with the topic of fallibility. When we acknowledge our fallibility with regard to the origin of the planets, we are not led to do so by the fear that we shall soon meet, face to face, the facts that attended their origin, as if these facts might belie our mental picture. We acknowledge our fallibility, rather, because we expect to find further *reasons*—reasons for or against our initial belief. It is these anticipated reasons, and not the facts attending the formation of the planets, that warn us against excessive confidence.

That being so, why is it necessary to become concerned about the corresponding situation in *ethics?* Why is it necessary, in the interest of encouraging our protestations of ethical fallibility, to postulate something "out there" that underlies our approvals? For if this something "out there" is to be an ethical analogue of a fact it will again be something that we shall not meet face to face; we shall not have to fear that our judgment will be belied by it. Or to change the metaphor, our approval cannot bruise its shins against an out-there value and become marked, thereby, as an approval that needs to be altered. All that actually serves to alter our approval (so far as observation and reflection have a role in this) is what I have called a body of reasons for approving or disapproving. These reasons do this, of course, only because they lead us to connect a given object of approval with other things, the latter too being objects of approval or disapproval. So, in effect, a given attitude is strengthened or held in check by the force of many other attitudes. But that is no more surprising than what we have, *mutatis mutandis*, in the sciences, where coherence tests lead one *belief* to be strengthened or held in check by many others.

Once again, then, there is an analogy between science and ethics; and although the shift from beliefs to attitudes, bringing with it a corresponding shift from reasons for believing or disbelieving to reasons for approving or disapproving, effectively prevents the analogy from becoming an identity, it leaves the analogy a sufficiently close one to establish my present point. Just as we can acknowledge, without half-heartedness and without caprice, a fallibility in science, bearing in mind that our conclusions may have to be revised in the light of further reasons for believing or disbelieving, so we can acknowledge, without half-heartedness and without caprice, a fallibility in ethics, bearing in mind that our conclusions may have to be revised in the light of further reasons for approving or disapproving. And in neither case does a postulation of something "out there," to be copied as a painter copies a model, increase or diminish our need of adding new reasons to our old ones.

Let me say just a little more about this, in the hope of avoiding a misunderstanding.

I am not suggesting that the term "fact" should always be viewed with suspicion. In many contexts it behaves quite as it should. There is nothing misleading, for instance, in the statement, "It is a fact that our planetary system was formed long ago"; for that is only a confident way of saying that our planetary system *was* formed long ago. But we have a different situation when a fact is described as "out there to be copied." That is misleading; and it is misleading because it gives us a confused conception of methodology. We are likely to suppose that our reasons for believing or disbelieving have only an *incidental* use in supporting or attacking our conclusion. The "final, important" step, we are tempted to feel, comes independently of that, and requires us to check our belief of the conclusion by comparing it with the fact. But this "final, important" step is nothing whatsoever.

And so it is, too, in ethics. The terms that are there similar to "fact"—such terms as "actual" value, "real" goodness, and "genuine" wrongness—are in most cases quite innocent. It is not misleading, for instance, to say, "Efforts to preserve the human race are *really* good"; for that is only a confident way of saying that efforts to preserve the human race are good. But what happens if we speak of actual or real or genuine values that are "out there to be copied"? We are again, as I see it, getting confused in our methodology. We are again looking for some "final, important" step—some step that will support or attack our judgment in a way that our reasons for approving or disapproving somehow half-fail to support or attack it. And this is also nothing whatsoever.

One might hope, of course, to *keep* the "out there" metaphor from being misleading, carefully separating it from the "to be copied" metaphor, and salvaging from it whatever turns out to be useful. But what can be salvaged, I suspect, will be disappointingly familiar. We speak of facts as "out there" to make clear that we are not, in discussing them, merely discussing our *beliefs about* them. (The beliefs, being mental, are "inside" this or that person, and so not "out there.") And of course some such distinction is needed; but it is rather less than exciting. It merely reminds us of a distinction that I made early in the paper: that a statement about the heavens, say, though it typically expresses a belief, is not about a belief. And the parallel between science and ethics continues to hold. If we should speak of an actual, real, or genuine value as being "out there" we should presumably be trying to make clear that we are evaluating something, and that we were *not* talking *about* our approval. And in the context of the present paper that distinction, I hope, can now be taken for granted. Value judgments are not about approval. They express and invite approval *as distinct from* being about it.

So much then, for the seeming connection between fallibility and the facts or values that are "out there" as models to be "copied." I wish I could say more in this connection; but the topic is so large that I must leave it, and bring my paper to a conclusion.

I cannot easily summarize my various remarks, so let me, instead, insist once more on my central theme. I have been saying, with regard to fallibility, what I said earlier with regard to language, uncertainty, disagreement, and reasoning—namely, that attitudes have much the same place in ethics as beliefs do in science. Nor is it possible, I think, to overemphasize this point. In contemporary philosophy, in spite of the new trends that have arisen since the war, we are still too much inclined to share what Santayana once called "the popular sense of the unworthiness and insignificance of things . . . emotional." We recoil, in particular, from attitudes, as if wishing that we could somehow transform them into beliefs. And that leaves us neither here nor there. The task of organizing and revising our attitudes is one that is constantly before us. If we fail to see this, claiming that our real task is concerned exclusively with the organization and revision of our beliefs, we shall thereby fail to *use* our beliefs to *guide* our attitudes. We shall explore many routes without intelligently selecting our destination.

ANCHOR BOOKS

PHILOSOPHY AND RELIGION

ALBRIGHT, WILLIAM FOXWELL   From the Stone Age to Christianity, A100

ALLEGRO, JOHN MARCO   The Treasure of the Copper Scroll, A412

ARENDT, HANNAH   The Human Condition, A182

BARRETT, WILLIAM   Irrational Man, A321

BARTH, KARL   Community, State and Church, A221

—— Evangelical Theology: An Introduction, A408

BENZ, ERNST   The Eastern Orthodox Church—Its Thought and Life, trans. Winston, A332

BERENSON, BERNARD   Aesthetics and History, A36

BERGSON, HENRI   *Laughter* (with Meredith's *Essay on Comedy*) in Comedy, A87

—— The Two Sources of Morality and Religion, A28

BROWN, ROBERT MC AFEE, & WEIGEL, GUSTAVE, S.J.   An American Dialogue, A257

BURKE, EDMUND   Edmund Burke: Selected Writings and Speeches, ed. Stanlis, A334

BURTT, E. A.   The Metaphysical Foundations of Modern Science, A41

CAMPBELL, EDWARD F., JR., & FREEDMAN, DAVID NOEL, eds.   The Biblical Archaeologist Reader, Vol. II, A250b

CARY, JOYCE   Art and Reality, A260

CASALIS, GEORGES   Portrait of Karl Barth, A422

CROSS, FRANK MOORE, JR.   The Ancient Library of Qumran, A272

FORSTER, E. M.   Alexandria: A History and a Guide, A231

FREUD, SIGMUND   The Future of an Illusion, A381

GALILEO   Discoveries and Opinions of Galileo, trans. Drake, A94

GASTER, THEODOR H.   The Dead Sea Scriptures (Revised edition), A378

GILKEY, LANGDON   Maker of Heaven and Earth, A442

GUSTAFSON, DONALD F., ed.   Essays in Philosophical Psychology, A417

HARRISON, G. B., ed.   The Bible for Students of Literature and Art, A394

HARTNACK, JUSTUS   Wittgenstein and Modern Philosophy, A469

HEIDEGGER, MARTIN   An Introduction to Metaphysics, A251

HERBERG, WILL, ed.   Four Existentialist Theologians, A141

—— Protestant-Catholic-Jew, A195

JASPERS, KARL   Man in the Modern Age, A101

KAUFMANN, WALTER   Critique of Religion and Philosophy, A252

—— The Faith of a Heretic, A336

—— From Shakespeare to Existentialism, A213

KIERKEGAARD, S.   Either/Or: 2 vols., A181a, A181b

—— Fear and Trembling *and* The Sickness unto Death, A30

KRAMER, SAMUEL NOAH, ed.   Mythologies of the Ancient World, A229

LEITH, JOHN H., ed.   Creeds of the Churches: A Reader in Christian Doctrine from the Bible to the Present, A312

LENSKI, GERHARD   The Religious Factor, A337

LEVENSON, JOSEPH R.   Modern China and Its Confucian Past: The Problem of Intellectual Continuity, A391

LITTELL, FRANKLIN H.   From State Church to Pluralism, A294

LUTHER, MARTIN   Martin Luther: Selections from His Writings, ed. Dillenberger, A271

MARX, KARL, & ENGELS, FRIEDRICH   Basic Writings on Politics and Philosophy, A185

A 7Aa

MEREDITH, GEORGE Essay on Comedy (with Bergson's *Laughter*) in Comedy, A87

MEYERHOFF, HANS, ed. The Philosophy of History in Our Time, A164

MUELLER, WILLIAM A. Church and State in Luther and Calvin, A454

MURRAY, GILBERT Five Stages of Greek Religion, A51

NEWMAN, JAMES R. Science and Sensibility, A357

NIETZSCHE, FRIEDRICH The Birth of Tragedy and The Genealogy of Morals, A81

ODAJNYK, WALTER Marxism and Existentialism, A443

ORTEGA Y GASSET, JOSE The Dehumanization of Art and Other Writings on Art and Culture, A72

PEEL, ROBERT Christian Science: Its Encounter with American Culture, A446

PLANTINGA, ALVIN, ed. The Ontological Argument, A435

PRABHAVANANDA, SWAMI, with FREDERICK MANCHESTER The Spiritual Heritage of India, A419

RAAB, EARL, ed. Religious Conflict in America: Studies of the Problem Beyond Bigotry, A392

RATHMELL, J. C. A., ed. The Psalms of Sir Philip Sidney and the Countess of Pembroke, A311

REPS, PAUL, ed. Zen Flesh, Zen Bones, A233

ROBINSON, JOAN Economic Philosophy, A415

ROSE, MARTIAL, ed. The Wakefield Mystery Plays, A371

RUSSELL, BERTRAND Mysticism and Logic, A104

SANTAYANA, GEORGE Three Philosophical Poets: Lucretius, Dante, Goethe, A17

SANTONI, RONALD, & SOMERVILLE, JOHN, eds. Social and Political Philosophy: Readings from Plato to Gandhi, A370

SCIAMA, D. W. The Unity of the Universe, A247

SIBLEY, MULFORD Q., ed. The Quiet Battle: Writings on the Theory and Practice of Non-Violent Resistance, A317

SIDNEY, SIR PHILIP The Psalms of Sir Philip Sidney and the Countess of Pembroke, ed. Rathmell, A311

SOMERVILLE, JOHN, & SANTONI, RONALD, eds. Social and Political Philosophy: Readings from Plato to Gandhi, A370

STANLIS, PETER J., ed. Edmund Burke: Selected Writings and Speeches, A334

STRAWSON, P. F. Individuals: An Essay in Descriptive Metaphysics, A364

SUZUKI, D. T. Zen Buddhism: Selected Writings of D. T. Suzuki, ed. Barrett, A90

SWARTZ, ROBERT J., ed. Perceiving, Sensing and Knowing, A460

TAYLOR, A. E. Socrates, A9

TAYLOR, RICHARD, ed. The Will to Live: Selected Writings of Arthur Schopenhauer, A266

VIDICH, ARTHUR J., & BENSMAN, JOSEPH Small Town in Mass Society: Class, Power and Religion in a Rural Community, A216

WALEY, ARTHUR Three Ways of Thought in Ancient China, A75

WILSON, EDMUND To the Finland Station, A6

WRIGHT, G. ERNEST, ed. The Bible and the Ancient Near East, A431

——, & FREEDMAN, DAVID NOEL, eds. The Biblical Archaeologist Reader, Vol. I, A250a

——, & FULLER, REGINALD The Book of the Acts of God, A222

ANCHOR BOOKS

SOCIOLOGY

ALLPORT, GORDON W. The Nature of Prejudice, A149
BARTH, KARL Community, State and Church, A221
BEDAU, HUGO ADAM, ed. The Death Penalty in America, A387
BELL, DANIEL The Radical Right, A376
BENDIX, REINHARD Max Weber: An Intellectual Portrait, A281
BERGER, MORROE The Arab World Today, A406
BERGER, PETER L. Invitation to Sociology: A Humanistic Perspective, A346
BROWN, ROBERT MC AFEE, & WEIGEL, GUSTAVE, S.J. An American Dialogue, A257
CABLE, GEORGE W. The Negro Question, A144
CAPLOW, THEODORE, & MC GEE, REECE J. The Academic Marketplace, A440
DARLING, F. FRASER A Herd of Red Deer, N35
DE GRAZIA, SEBASTIAN Of Time, Work and Leisure, A380
DOLLARD, JOHN Caste and Class in a Southern Town, A95
ERIKSON, ERIK H., ed. The Challenge of Youth, A438
FICHTER, JOSEPH H. Parochial School: A Sociological Study, A420
FORTUNE, EDITORS OF The Exploding Metropolis, A146
FREEDMAN, RONALD, ed. Population: The Vital Revolution, A423
GATHERU, MUGO Child of Two Worlds, A468
GOFFMAN, ERVING Asylums: Essays on the Social Situation of Mental Patients and Other Inmates, A277
——— The Presentation of Self in Everyday Life, A174
GRANICK, DAVID The European Executive, A397
——— The Red Executive: A Study of the Organization Man in Russian Industry, A246
HACKER, ANDREW Corporation Take-Over, A465
HANDLIN, OSCAR The Newcomers, A283
——— Race and Nationality in American Life, A110
HENDIN, HERBERT Suicide and Scandinavia, A457
HERBERG, WILL Protestant-Catholic-Jew, A195
HOOVER, EDGAR M., & VERNON, RAYMOND Anatomy of a Metropolis, A298
HUNTER, FLOYD Community Power Structure, A379
JONES, ERNEST The Life and Work of Sigmund Freud, ed. & abr. in 1 vol. Trilling & Marcus, A340

A 9Aa

ANCHOR BOOKS

PSYCHOLOGY

A 10a

ANCHOR BOOKS